NEW DIRECTIONS FOR PROGRAM EVALUATION
A Publication of the American Evaluation Association

William R. Shadish, *Memphis State University*
EDITOR-IN-CHIEF

A15046 835298

Preventing the Misuse of Evaluation

Carla J. Stevens
Evaluation & Data Analysis Services Inc.

Micah Dial
Evaluation & Data Analysis Services Inc.

EDITORS

Number 64, Winter 1994

JOSSEY-BASS PUBLISHERS
San Francisco

PREVENTING THE MISUSE OF EVALUATION
Carla J. Stevens, Micah Dial (eds.)
New Directions for Program Evaluation, no. 64
William R. Shadish, Editor-in-Chief

Microfilm copies of issues and articles are available in 16mm and 35mm, as well as microfiche in 105mm, through University Microfilms Inc., 300 North Zeeb Road, Ann Arbor, Michigan 48106-1346.

LC 85-644749   ISSN 0164-7989   ISBN 0-7879-9993-8

NEW DIRECTIONS FOR PROGRAM EVALUATION is part of The Jossey-Bass Education Series and is published quarterly by Jossey-Bass Inc., Publishers, 350 Sansome Street, San Francisco, California 94104-1342.

Subscriptions for 1994 cost $54.00 for individuals and $75.00 for institutions, agencies, and libraries.

EDITORIAL CORRESPONDENCE should be sent to the Editor-in-Chief, William R. Shadish, Department of Psychology, Memphis State University, Memphis, Tennessee 38152.

Manufactured in the United States of America. Nearly all Jossey-Bass books, jackets, and periodicals are printed on recycled paper that contains at least 50 percent recycled waste, including 10 percent postconsumer waste. Many of our materials are also printed with vegetable-based inks; during the printing process, these inks emit fewer volatile organic compounds (VOCs) than petroleum-based inks. VOCs contribute to the formation of smog.

Editorial Policy and Procedures

New Directions for Program Evaluation (NDPE), a quarterly sourcebook, is an official publication of the American Evaluation Association. NDPE publishes empirical, methodological, and theoretical works on all aspects of evaluation and related fields. Substantive areas may include any program, field, or issue with which evaluation is concerned, such as government performance, tax policy, energy, environment, mental health, education, job training, medicine, and public health. Also included are such topics as product evaluation, personnel evaluation, policy analysis, and technology assessment. In all cases, the focus on evaluation is more important than the substantive topics. We are particularly interested in encouraging a diversity of evaluation perspectives and experiences and in expanding the boundaries of our field beyond the evaluation of social programs.

NDPE does not consider or publish unsolicited single manuscripts. Each issue of NDPE is devoted to a single topic, with contributions solicited, organized, reviewed, and edited by a guest editor. Issues may take any of several forms, such as a series of related chapters, a debate, or a long article followed by brief critical commentaries. In all cases, the proposals must follow a specific format, which can be obtained from the editor-in-chief. These proposals are sent to members of the editorial board and to relevant substantive experts for peer review. The process may result in acceptance, a recommendation to revise and resubmit, or rejection. However, NDPE is committed to working constructively with potential guest editors to help them develop acceptable proposals.

Lois-ellin Datta, Editor-in-Chief
P.O. Box 383768
Waikoloa, HI 96738

Jennifer C. Greene, Associate Editor
Department of Human Service Studies
Cornell University
Ithaca, NY 14853-4401

Gary Henry, Associate Editor
Public Administration and Urban Studies
Georgia State University
Atlanta, GA 30302-4039

CONTENTS

Editors' Notes

The purpose of this issue is to discuss the misuse of evaluation. Conner (1988) wrote, "My interest in utilization has a very practical beginning: it arose from my discouragement in seeing the results of some of my evaluation work go unused" (p. 274) and "[a]fter nearly a decade and a half of work on refining the goals and methods of evaluation, evaluation researchers still frequently face the unpleasant reality that the fruits of their hard labors—the evaluation study results—are not used or are misused" (p. 273). Such sentiments are also the reason for our interest in the topic of evaluation misuse. Although evaluation use is a more popular topic, we find that evaluators have in fact mentioned misuse for some time (Raizen and Rossi, 1981; Alkin and Coyle, 1988) and, in speaking with others for this project, we found that it is a common concern among evaluators.

All of the contributions in this volume recount experiences of evaluators in which the evaluation process or the evaluation findings were misused. The reader will find that the emphasis of each is not on discussing concepts or tracing the history of misuse. Rather, the authors tell their own stories of misuse. There are two findings that may interest readers. First, in each account, the problems surrounding misuse are usually not methodological issues. Instead, misuse is an issue of human relations and often of political pressure. Second, these chapters relate situations with which an evaluator can identify. Two of the chapters are from the field of criminal justice, two are from social work, one is from psychology, and two are from education. Unfortunately, experiences with misuse appear to be common to all fields.

This issue begins with the guest editors' framework for evaluation misuse, which considers the definition of misuse. In Chapter Two, Dennis Palumbo discusses the political roots of misuse. Because evaluations are conducted in a political arena, evaluators must consider their roles as decision makers and policy makers as well as their role as technicians.

In Chapter Three, Barbara Poitras Duffy discusses the experience of an internal evaluation unit where attempts from within the organization were made to alter the evaluation. In this particular case, the position of the evaluation department within the organization helped to prevent misuse.

Chapter Four, by Carol Mowbray, recounts an experience in which a state internal evaluation division was incrementally dissolved. Mowbray states that the decisions made in a political environment may not always be what would otherwise be considered rational.

Chapter Five, by Phyllis Vroom, Marie Colombo, and Neva Nahan, recounts the experience of an external evaluation team in which there was a blatant attempt to cover the lack of work by an almost nonexistent program. The authors list suggestions to help avoid such situations.

Chapter Six, by Micah Dial, presents scenarios from the field of education. The conclusion is that misuse of an evaluation occurs when one alters the process or the findings to promote self-interests, and that this generally occurs because programs have difficulty showing a positive impact on their targeted populations.

Emil Posavac, in Chapter Seven, discusses a misuse of evaluation in which the wrong question is asked. According to the author, program personnel's lack of understanding of evaluation leads to requesting one type of evaluation (summative, in this case) when another type (formative) is needed.

To conclude this issue, an interview with a sponsor and user of evaluations in the field of education is transcribed by Carla Stevens in Chapter Eight. We think readers will find it interesting to hear from the other side. The user defines misuse as asking the wrong research questions, but puts the onus on the evaluators instead of program personnel. The ideas are well-articulated and are a fitting conclusion to this volume on evaluation misuse.

Carla J. Stevens
Micah Dial
Editors

References

Alkin, M. C., and Coyle, K. "Thoughts on Evaluation Utilization, Misutilization, and Non-utilization." *Studies in Educational Evaluation,* 1988, *14,* 331–340.
Conner, R. F. "Structuring Knowledge Production Activities to Facilitate Knowledge Utilization: Thoughts on Important Utilization Issues." *Studies in Educational Evaluation,* 1988, *14,* 273–283.
Raizen, S. A., and Rossi, P. H. (eds.). *Program Evaluation in Education: When? How? To What Ends?* Washington, D.C.: National Academy Press, 1981.

CARLA J. STEVENS *is president of Evaluation & Data Analysis Services, Inc., in Houston, Texas.*

MICAH DIAL *is senior research consultant for Evaluation & Data Analysis Services, Inc., in Houston, Texas.*

This introductory chapter offers a discussion of evaluation misuse, including ways in which evaluations and their results may be misused, by whom, and for what reasons.

What Constitutes Misuse?

Carla J. Stevens, Micah Dial

Program evaluation became widely used in the 1950s (Berk, 1981). Since that time, evaluators have continued to debate the evaluator's role and methods for improving the use of evaluation (Leviton and Hughes, 1979, 1981; Patton, 1988; Rossi and Freeman, 1982; Shadish, Cook, and Leviton, 1991). However, little has been written directly discussing the misuse of evaluation. For years, it has remained an informal topic of discussion among evaluators, often with the relaying of a personal experience. Although there have been articles that mention evaluation misuse in passing, few publications have focused solely on this topic. The chapters in this volume are intended to stimulate evaluators' awareness of the critical need for methods to address some of the ethical issues and implications underlying evaluation misuse.

Definition of Misuse

In order to discuss misuse, it must first be defined. The World Book Dictionary defines misuse as "*n.* A wrong or improper use; misapplication. *v.* 1. To use for the wrong purpose; use improperly. 2. To abuse; ill-treat; mistreat." A misuser is defined as one who "1. Unlawfully uses a liberty, benefit, or power. 2. A person who misuses." Within this context, the misuse of evaluation means that an evaluation has been used for the wrong purpose or that the results of an evaluation have been misapplied or used improperly.

According to Chelimsky (1983), "The concept of usefulness . . . depends upon the perspective and values of the observer. This means that one person's usefulness may be another person's waste" (p. 155). This interpretation also applies to the concept of misuse. What one evaluator or stakeholder considers misuse, another may find appropriate. Also, what constitutes misuse in one situation may be appropriate in another. Alkin and Coyle (1988) present the hypothetical situation in which a stakeholder blatantly squashes a negative evaluation so that the results will not become public. At first glance, this appears to be a classic case of misuse. However, if the report were invalid due to poor data collection methods, would the intentional burying of this report be an appropriate action?

Alkin and Coyle (1988) define misuse as "the intentional (and even malicious) manipulation of some aspect of an evaluation (evaluative results, for example) in order to gain something, position or support, for instance" (p. 334). They make the distinction between misuse, nonuse, and misevaluation, or flawed evaluation. They place the responsibility for misuse on the users, while the responsibility for what they term misevaluation lies with evaluators.

According to Patton (1988), evaluation use and evaluation misuse are not opposites of each other. Rather, they are different dimensions. "One dimension is a continuum from nonutilization to utilization. A second continuum is non-misutilization to misutilization" (p. 327). He further proposes that *as utilization increases, misutilization will also increase* (p. 327, italics in original). Thus, as evaluations provide more useful information, there will be a greater potential for abuse.

It can be strongly argued, however, that nonuse of an evaluation may indeed be a misuse of the evaluation and may negatively affect the program participants. Furthermore, the creation of useless evaluations may be a misuse of the evaluation process and resources, and may lead to further mistrust of evaluations on the part of stakeholders.

If this is true, one must also have a cursory understanding of evaluation use. As noted above, a great deal has been written about the use of evaluations and evaluation results. Shadish, Cook, and Leviton (1991) present a thorough discussion on evaluation use and the components of what they would consider a "good theory of use." "A good theory of use comprehensively discusses possible kinds of use, time frames in which use occurs, and things evaluators do to facilitate use" (p. 54). They also identify three types of use of evaluations: instrumental use—making direct decisions regarding programs based on evaluation results; conceptual use—affecting how people think about an issue (also known as enlightenment or demystification); and persuasive use—using evaluation results to persuade people of a position already taken.

Shadish, Cook, and Leviton also address evaluation misuse in regard to the type of use, specifically instrumental use. The misuse of evaluation may arise in situations, or because of situations, that they describe as obstacles to instrumental use. These obstacles are as follows:

> Evaluative results often threaten entrenched interests.
> Social programs *as a whole* rarely die or get replaced.
> Service deliverers engage in practices for reasons besides efficacy,
>   such as convenience, habit, and security.

Political decision making is a slow process, and change is almost always incremental.

Policy makers and managers use information in many ways.

If an innovation is highly successful, local personnel may still not adopt it.

[1991, pp. 54–55]

Evaluation Standards. Because one of the definitions of misuse is wrong or improper use, a method that can be applied to determining whether something is being used improperly is to compare it to standards in the industry. If the agreed-upon standards define how something is to be conducted, used, or applied, then not to follow the standards could be considered misuse. The educational evaluation field has recently released the newly revised *The Program Evaluation Standards, 2nd Edition: How to Assess Evaluations of Educational Programs* (Joint Committee on Standards for Educational Evaluation, 1994). The thirty standards are broken down into four categories: utility, feasibility, propriety, and accuracy. The utility standards address the importance of serving the "information needs of the intended users" (p. 23). In accordance with the feasibility standards, program evaluation should be "realistic, prudent, diplomatic, and frugal" (p. 63). The propriety standards address the legal and ethical responsibilities of an evaluator to respect those who may be affected by an evaluation. The last set of standards, accuracy, refers to the technical quality of an evaluation with regard to how it assesses the worth or merit of a program.

Although the misuse of an evaluation could be the result of not adhering as diligently as possible to any of the evaluation standards, only nine of the thirty standards are discussed here. These nine pertain most directly to situations of evaluation misuse depicted in the remaining chapters of this volume. These standards are as follows:

U1: Stakeholder Identification. Persons involved in or affected by the evaluation should be identified so that their needs can be addressed.

U3: Information Scope and Selection. Information collected should be broadly selected to address pertinent questions about the program and be responsive to the needs and interests of clients and other specified stakeholders.

U7: Evaluation Impact. Evaluations should be planned, conducted, and reported in ways that encourage follow-through by stakeholders so that the likelihood that the evaluation will be used is increased.

F2: Political Viability. The evaluation should be planned and conducted with anticipation of the different positions of various interest groups so that their cooperation may be obtained and so that possible attempts by any of these groups to curtail evaluation operations or to bias or misapply the results can be averted or counteracted.

P2: Formal Agreements. Obligations of the formal parties to an evaluation (what is to be done, how, by whom, when) should be agreed to in writing so that these parties are obligated to adhere to all conditions of the agreement or to formally renegotiate it.

P5: Complete and Fair Assessment. The evaluation should be complete and fair in its examination and recording of strengths and weaknesses of the program being evaluated so that strengths can be built on and problem areas addressed.

P6: Disclosure of Findings. The formal parties to an evaluation should ensure that the full set of evaluation findings along with pertinent limitations are made accessible to the persons affected by the evaluation and any others with expressed legal rights to receive the results.

P7: Conflict of Interest. Conflict of interest should be dealt with openly and honestly so that it does not compromise the evaluation processes and results.

A11: Impartial Reporting. Reporting procedures should guard against distortion caused by personal feelings and biases of any party to the evaluation so that evaluation reports fairly reflect the evaluation findings.

Guidelines as to how best to apply the standards and common errors made regarding each standard are also detailed in *The Program Evaluation Standards.* The guidelines provide evaluators with proactive methods for avoiding some types of evaluation misuse within evaluators' control.

There are many ways in which evaluation misuse may be defined. Furthermore, there are many ways in which evaluations may be misused, by different stakeholders (including the evaluator) and for different reasons. Each of these areas along with suggestions for ways to avoid misuse will be discussed in the following sections of this chapter, in light of the case studies presented by the authors in this issue.

What Constitutes Misuse?

The misuse of evaluations may take various forms. It may also occur at different stages in the evaluation process. Alkin and Coyle (1988) divide types of misuse into three categories based on when in the evaluation process the misuse typically occurs. These categories are misuse of commissioning an evaluation; misuse of the evaluation process; and misuse of evaluative findings.

Misuse of Commissioning an Evaluation. Misuse may occur at the beginning of the evaluation process. This occurs when the evaluation is designed such that the results will be inappropriate for the proper use of the evaluation report or final product. This type of misuse may also occur when the evaluator has a preconceived agenda regarding evaluation outcomes and designs an evaluation plan that will produce only the desired results.

Evaluation misuse at the beginning of the evaluation process may also occur when stakeholders exert power over the evaluator to design an evaluation that will serve their own political or personal interests and that may not be in the best interest of the program staff or program participants. Duffy, in Chapter Three, and Dial, in Chapter Six, describe situations of potential misuse of internal evaluations by an organization's executive management. In

Duffy's case, the evaluation is commissioned solely to give the appearance of objectively assessing issues, policies, and programs when, in fact, decisions already have been reached. The opposite situation occurred for Dial when a negative evaluation was requested to support an administrator's position regarding a program.

Another example of misuse at this point in the evaluation process may be when stakeholders unintentionally request that a certain type of evaluation be conducted. For example, a summative evaluation may be requested when what is really needed is a formative one. If the evaluator continues with the summative design and does not question how the results would be used, then conducting a useless evaluation results in a misuse of the evaluation process and of the evaluator's and program staff's time and resources. Examples of this type of evaluation misuse are presented by Posavac in Chapter Seven and Stevens in Chapter Eight.

Misuse of the Evaluation Process. Examples of misuse of the evaluation process include using evaluations to delay actions and using evaluations to avoid taking responsibility (Alkin and Coyle, 1988). Interfering with the data collection process is another type of misuse at this stage.

Several case studies describing this second type of evaluation misuse are presented by Vroom, Colombo, and Nahan (Chapter Five), Duffy, and Dial. In all of these cases, stakeholders interfered with data collection efforts in order to influence the results of the evaluation. In Duffy's chapter, misuse resulted from management's coaching respondents, leaking incorrect information to other stakeholders, and attempting to exert personal influence over the evaluator. Vroom, Colombo, and Nahan describe attempts by program leadership and program staff to manage information about program operation through the exaggeration of the number of participants and the number of active program sites, missed appointments, lack of record keeping, and failure to supply data and documents. A similar situation occurred for Dial with an uncooperative program director.

Misuse of the Evaluative Findings. Most frequently, misuse is thought of as one of the stakeholders attempting to change the evaluation results to fit his or her own agenda. One approach is when stakeholders present the data, or demand that the data be presented, in a more negative fashion so that the program will be canceled, even though participants may be receiving the desired results. The other is when stakeholders whitewash the results, deleting any negative findings so that the program will be continued, even though participants may not be benefiting from the program at all.

Other examples of misuse at this stage of the evaluation may include selectively reporting the results, ascribing findings to a study that differ from the actual results, inaccurately transmitting results, and oversimplifying findings (Alkin and Coyle, 1988). They may also include using the results to further a political career, or to end one; using results to reward or punish staff; or not distributing findings to other stakeholders.

In Chapter Two of this volume, Palumbo presents a case study wherein the evaluator changes the results of an evaluation report in order to satisfy the client. He argues, however, that if by dropping some of the findings that the client finds objectionable the evaluator is able to help promote or further the prospects of the continuation of a program that the evaluator believes in and finds to be worthwhile, it is not a misuse of the evaluation. This conflicts directly, however, with the Program Evaluation Standards discussed earlier in this chapter. Standards P5 and A11 hold that evaluations should be complete in the reporting of strengths and weaknesses of the program being evaluated and that the reporting procedures should guard against distortion caused by personal feelings and biases of any party to the evaluation.

Dial presents a scenario in which the evaluator applied differential treatment in the evaluation of two programs, neither of which complied with federally mandated structure and rules, yet one appeared to be serving its target population while the other did not. Misuse occurs if one program is rewarded or recognized over another solely because of personal or political similarities between the program personnel and the evaluator, and not because of desired effects on program participants.

Another misuse of evaluative findings may take the form of a client rejecting the findings or blatantly ignoring the results. Weiss (1973) states that "devastating evidence of program failure has left some policies and programs unscathed, and positive evidence has not shielded others from dissolution" (p. 40). Palumbo describes a situation in which a program continued and even was expanded, yet the evaluation report indicated that the program had no effect on participants.

Who Misuses Evaluations?

If, as stated earlier, a misuser is defined as one who unlawfully uses a liberty, benefit, or power, then any stakeholder of a program evaluation may potentially misuse either the evaluation process or the results. Stakeholders are "individuals or groups who may affect or be affected by program evaluation" (Joint Committee on Standards for Educational Evaluation, 1994, p. 209). These groups or individuals may enjoy liberties, benefits, or power generated by the program evaluation that could be either unlawfully or, most commonly, unethically misused.

Rossi and Freeman (1982) present a detailed but not completely exhaustive list of possible stakeholders. This list includes the following:

Policy makers and decision makers. Individuals responsible for deciding whether a program is to be instituted, continued, discontinued, expanded, or curtailed.
Program sponsor. Organization that initiates and funds the program.
Evaluation sponsor. Organization that initiates and funds the evaluation. (Sometimes the evaluation sponsor and the program sponsor are the same stakeholder.)

Target participants. Individuals, households, or other units who participate in the program or receive the intervention services under evaluation.

Program management. Group responsible for overseeing and coordinating the program.

Program staff. Personnel responsible for actual delivery of the intervention (such as teachers).

Evaluators. Group or individuals responsible for the design or conduct of the evaluation.

Program competitors. Organizations or groups who compete for resources.

Contextual stakeholders. Organizations, groups, individuals, and other units in the immediate environment of a program (such as local government officials or influentials situated on or near the program site).

The chapters in this volume give examples of misuse by some of these different stakeholders. Case studies in which policy makers and decision makers misuse evaluations are detailed by Palumbo, Duffy, and Dial. In one case, the decision makers ignored negative evaluation findings and expanded the politically supported program. In another case, the decision makers commissioned an evaluation even though decisions had already been made. In the third case, a negative evaluation was requested to support the administrator's stance on the program. Palumbo also presents a case where the evaluation and program sponsor objected to negative findings in the evaluation report and requested that they be removed. Further misuse may have occurred when the evaluator changed the results in order to satisfy the client.

For Posavac, the misusers were evaluation sponsors who wanted to learn more about their programs but requested summative evaluations. By dictating a program evaluation design that would be useless, the evaluation sponsors misused the evaluation process. The evaluator also misused the evaluation by not ascertaining exactly how the information provided would be used and by not educating the evaluation sponsor regarding a more appropriate type of evaluation design. This type of misuse by the evaluator is also discussed by Stevens, where the evaluator did not work with the program people to create appropriate research questions that actually reflected program operations.

Actual and attempted misuse conducted by program management and program staff are discussed in Chapters Three, Five, and Six. In one case, program management attempted to sway the evaluation by coaching interview respondents, trying to co-opt members of the evaluation team, and spreading false information about the evaluation team to stakeholders on the opposing side of the issue. Vroom, Colombo, and Nahan experienced a situation in which program management and staff provided misleading information, were evasive, and failed to provide requested information. The evaluators were led to believe that a program was in the implementation stage, when actually it was still in the planning phase. In Dial's case, the program director repeatedly tried to stop an evaluation that presented two recommendations that reflected negatively on her.

Why are Evaluations Misused?

Are all misuses intentional and political in nature? Are such actions always driven by self-preservation? As Rossi and Freeman (1982) note, evaluation "is not just a technical activity . . . it is also a political activity" (p. 301). They go on to state that "evaluations always are conducted within contexts in which there are many interested parties with stakes in the outcomes of the efforts" (p. 301). In discussing the political nature of evaluation, Shadish, Cook, and Leviton (1991, p. 223) cite Hedrick (1988), who notes that although politics can be a positive force in evaluation, she agrees that it interferes with evaluation in many ways. Some ways in which politics can hinder an evaluation are as follows:

> Political pressure may be exerted in ways that bias the scope of evaluation research.
> Political pressure may be exerted to press for unrealistic time frames for completion of research.
> Political pressure may be exerted on evaluators to distort study results.
> Political entities may disseminate or use evaluation results selectively.
> Political pressure may suppress the release of an evaluation report. [Hedrick, 1988, pp. 7–8]

Stakeholders can have a positive or negative influence on the evaluation process and its results. Thus, there may be as many reasons for evaluation misuse as there are types of misuse and misusers. Some of these reasons for evaluation misuse or potential misuse are also discussed by the authors in this volume.

Palumbo describes a situation in which strong political support for a program persuaded stakeholders to expand a program, even though the evaluation found that the program had no effect on the participants. Evaluation sponsors may also exert power over evaluators in an attempt to change evaluation results, thereby serving their own interests. Furthermore, evaluators may misuse evaluations and provide results to accommodate the evaluation sponsors in order to get additional contracts. Palumbo argues, however, that it is not misuse if the evaluator, acting as an involved stakeholder, accommodates other stakeholders in order to remain in a discourse coalition and influence the direction of policy and programs he or she believes are worthwhile.

Duffy also addresses this issue in her discussion of attempted misuse of internal evaluation by executive management as being politically motivated and serving the interests of those attempting to misuse the evaluation, regardless of what is in the best interests of all the stakeholders. Vroom, Colombo, and Nahan (Chapter Five) and Dial (Chapter Six) attribute evaluation misuse by program management and staff to self-interest focused on project survival. In the one case study, if the funding sources discovered that the program never really had entered the implementation stage, the money would have been withdrawn (which eventually it was). In the other situation, the program director was covering up alleged improprieties conducted for self-gain.

Mowbray (Chapter Four) discusses evaluation misuse from a more global perspective. Her case study describes the gradual elimination of an internal evaluation department due to a politicized environment. Politically and fiscally motivated decision making shifts the emphasis of the social service agency away from a strong evaluation component.

What Can Evaluators and Users Do to Prevent Misuse of Evaluations?

It can be argued that the ultimate stakeholders in the consequences of social policy and program outcomes, be it in health and human services, criminal justice, education, psychology, or social services, are the target populations— those being served.

What Can Be Done? Each of the authors in this issue provides suggestions to evaluators on how to avoid certain types of evaluation misuse. In the case where stakeholders ask the wrong questions and request an inappropriate type of evaluation, Posavac encourages evaluators to take an active role in helping clients to understand exactly what they need. He lists several steps to remedy this type of misuse. First, educate clients on the various types of evaluations and the purpose of each. Second, ask clients how they might use an evaluation and the evaluation results. Third, suggest possible outcomes of an evaluation. This will help both evaluators and stakeholders match the evaluation design to the needs of program managers and staff, thus averting the misuse of resources. Stevens places the responsibility on the evaluator not only to be present during program and evaluation planning, but to take an active role in directing the program personnel to ask appropriate, measurable research questions regarding changes that honestly can be expected from the target population.

Palumbo addresses two types of evaluation misuse and how to avoid such problems. In cases where misuse is the client ignoring evaluation results, however, he holds that "there is little, if anything, an evaluator can do to correct the misuse (other than to publish the results in a scholarly journal)." Nevertheless, Shadish, Cook, and Leviton (1991) provide a list of activities that may facilitate the instrumental use of evaluations. These include "identifying users early in the evaluation; having frequent contact with users, especially during question formation; studying things that users can control; providing interim results; translating findings into actions; and disseminating results through informal meetings, oral briefings, media presentations, and final reports with brief and nontechnical executive summaries" (p. 55). Even when an evaluator follows such practices, political influences can still result in evaluation misuse. Thus, as long as the evaluator has done everything within his or her power to make the evaluation useful to the client, and if the client's decision not to use the evaluation is politically motivated, Palumbo may be right in concluding that the situation is often out of the evaluator's control.

To resolve the situation where a client objects to certain evaluation findings and requests that they be dropped, Palumbo suggests that, as an active stakeholder, an evaluator may compromise with another stakeholder only if it helps promote or continue a program the evaluator believes to be worthwhile. If the evaluator does not believe in the program, then he or she should not eliminate negative results. Furthermore, Dial suggests that evaluators should make a conscious effort to question themselves periodically regarding how their personal preferences may be influencing evaluation results.

For an internal evaluation department, it is difficult to avoid attempted misuse by executive directors within the organization. Nevertheless, Duffy offers some suggestions, both within the evaluator's control and outside of the evaluator's control. As organization members, evaluators have insider knowledge of the politics at play. Being aware of the situation, they may be able to avoid pressures or attempts at persuasion before they happen. Evaluators may also use multiple data sources, include additional stakeholders in data collection efforts to emphasize the neutrality of the evaluation staff, and use focus groups to promote openness surrounding the issues under consideration.

Another method by which internal evaluators can avoid misuse and abuse of the evaluation process and results is to have the evaluation unit report directly to the head of the organization. Such is the case Duffy describes where the organizational placement of evaluation puts it where no departmental executive managers or directors have power over it. As suggested by Dial, an internal evaluation department at a school district would best be used if it reported directly to the superintendent of schools or even directly to the school board. He also makes a strong argument for using external evaluators to avoid internal politics.

Vroom, Colombo, and Nahan give hindsight recommendations as to how evaluators could avoid misuse of the evaluation process by program management and staff. Based on their case study, it is recommended that evaluators formally present the evaluability assessment to the program leadership; insist on meeting periodically with program leadership collectively; determine exactly who is in charge of making decisions; make explicit that changes in the program and program emphasis may affect the evaluation; and confront immediately any perceived evasion by program leaders of evaluator efforts to collect data.

As can be seen by the variety of advice given by the authors in this issue, much of it is case-specific. Different remedies apply to different types of misuse by different stakeholders, some of which are in the evaluator's control and some of which are not. A further recommendation is for evaluators to be familiar with the Program Evaluation Standards and to adhere to them as closely as possible. Although this will not eliminate misuse completely, evaluators will be better prepared to handle typical cases of attempted misuse by stakeholders and to avoid any intentional misuse by evaluators themselves.

This introduction to the topic of evaluation misuse is by no means exhaustive. The intention here was to begin a formal discourse on ways in which evaluations and their results may be misused, by whom, and for what reasons. It is up to evaluators to continue to expose ways in which evaluations have been, or can be, misused, and to explore ways in which these attempts can be thwarted. As long as our society continues to believe that information is power and that evaluations provide useful information, there will be those who want to control it and use it for their own purposes, which may not be in the best interests of those who supposedly are being served.

References

Alkin, M. C., and Coyle, K. "Thoughts on Evaluation Utilization, Misutilization and Non-utilization." *Studies in Educational Evaluation,* 1988, *14,* 331–340.
Berk, R. A. (ed.). *Educational Evaluation Methodology: The State of the Art.* Baltimore: The Johns Hopkins University Press, 1981.
Chelimsky, E. "Improving the Cost Effectiveness of Evaluation." In M. C. Alkin and L. C. Solmon (eds.), *The Costs of Evaluation.* Newbury Park, Calif.: Sage, 1983.
Hedrick, T. E. "The Interaction of Politics and Evaluation." *Evaluation Practice,* 1988, *9,* 5–14.
The Joint Committee on Standards for Educational Evaluation. *The Program Evaluation Standards.* 2nd ed. Newbury Park, Calif.: Sage, 1994.
Leviton, L. C., and Hughes, E.F.X. *Utilization of Evaluations.* Evanston, Ill.: Northwestern University Center for Health Services and Policy Research, 1979.
Leviton, L. C., and Hughes, E.F.X. "Research on the Utilization of Evaluations: A Review and Synthesis." *Evaluation Review,* 1981, *5,* 525–548.
Patton, M. Q. "Six Honest Serving Men for Evaluation." *Studies in Educational Evaluation,* 1988, *14,* 301–330.
Rossi, P. H., and Freeman, H. E. *Evaluation: A Systematic Approach.* Newbury Park, Calif.: Sage, 1982.
Shadish, W. R., Jr., Cook, T. D., and Leviton, L. C. (eds.). *Foundations of Program Evaluation: Theories of Practice.* Newbury Park, Calif.: Sage, 1991.
Weiss, C. H. "Where Politics and Evaluation Research Meet." *Evaluation,* 1973, *1,* 37–45.

CARLA J. STEVENS is president of Evaluation & Data Analysis Services, Inc., in Houston, Texas.

MICAH DIAL is senior research consultant for Evaluation & Data Analysis Services, Inc., in Houston, Texas.

Two types of evaluation misuse are described: misuse by a client who is politically committed to continuing or expanding a program regardless of the results; and misuse by an evaluator who changes results in order to satisfy the client.

The Political Roots of Misuse of Evaluation

Dennis J. Palumbo

Assume that you are an evaluator who has turned in an evaluation report to a committee that is your client. Some members of the committee are dissatisfied with portions of the report that make the program look as if it will fail. One member says, "If this gets out, we will not be funded by the legislature next year." The client asks that you remove these portions. What would you do?

The apparent ethical answer is to refuse to remove the offending portions. However, ethics is not black or white but many shades of gray. The answer is not as simple as it seems, especially considering arguments some analysts (Fischer and Forester, 1993; Majone, 1989) have made about the role of evaluators in policy making. I will discuss this later in this chapter. First, I will discuss two types of possible misuse of evaluations, then a specific case in which I was involved that posed the dilemma described above, and finally, the role of evaluators in policy making.

Misuse by the Client

No doubt, most evaluators would say that if the evaluator removed the parts of the evaluation that made the program look bad, thus biasing the results, it would be a misuse of evaluation. That is one type of misuse, and perhaps not the principal type. Misuses of evaluation can take several forms. The most obvious is when those who solicit an evaluation distort the findings or simply reject the findings and ignore the evaluation. This latter may be the reason why many evaluations do not get used; they come up with negative results and it is politically necessary for the client to ignore them. Indeed, if Rossi's Iron Law of Evaluation is true, evaluations might never be used. Rossi (1985, p. 2) states, "The expected value of any net impact assessment of any social program is zero. That means that our best a priori estimate of a net impact assessment of a program is that it will have no effect. It also means that the average of net impact assessments of a large set of social programs will crawl asymptotically toward zero."

However, as Shadish, Cook, and Leviton (1991) note, not all programs fail to have at least some positive results. In cases where an evaluation turns up negative results and is ignored, however, the misuse is on the part of the client rather than the evaluator. This has happened in one evaluation in which I was involved—an evaluation of Gang Resistance Education and Training (GREAT).

The GREAT program involves uniformed police officers conducting eight one-hour sessions with seventh-grade students over the course of eight weeks. The purpose is to change children's attitudes about gangs in the hope that this will deter them from joining gangs. The evaluation I conducted showed that it did not have any impact on children's attitudes about gangs and, therefore, possibly no impact on their decision to join or quit a gang. Of course, it is unlikely that such limited exposure to an antigang curriculum would have any impact on the attitudes or behavior of seventh-graders, especially because the classes were conducted by police officers, not expert teachers.

Nevertheless, the GREAT program has powerful political support (primarily from the Bureau of Alcohol, Tobacco, and Firearms and the police who conduct it) and a negative evaluation is not sufficient to prevent it from continuing. Although the evaluation showed that GREAT does not have the desired impact, it suggested ways that it might be improved. Focus groups conducted at a dozen schools with groups of twelve students who participated in GREAT showed that the officers might be more effective if they did not say that all gangs and gang members were delinquents. This is because many of the children were members of gangs, were "wannabes," or had friends who were members of gangs. Also, the students were more positive about the program when they were allowed to participate in role playing rather than just listening to a lecture.

The program director made changes in year two that reflected these process findings, but the evaluation in year two again found that the program was not changing children's attitudes about gangs. However, in classes where the officers were more friendly and accessible, the students had more positive feelings about officers, which correlated with more negative feelings about gangs. Thus, it is possible that, if the classes were done right, there might be a positive impact because the children might have more positive feelings about police. The evaluation also found that although the majority of children had positive feelings about police and negative feelings about gangs, a substantial minority had the opposite feelings. (This was determined using a "feeling thermometer.") The research also identified the ethnic background of the children who were more negative about officers and positive about gangs. These tended to be children of Hispanic or Latino background. Other research indicates that gangs are a cultural tradition among these groups (Spergel, 1991) and thus it is unlikely that their attitudes could be easily changed, particularly by such limited training. Nevertheless, if Hispanic officers were used as the teachers, there might possibly be more positive feelings among these students.

Although the results of the evaluation each year showed that students' attitudes about gangs did not change, the program is continuing. It is not only continuing, but expanding to many other states. Four points emerge from this particular experience:

Programs that have powerful political support will be continued no matter what the evaluation shows.
Even though an evaluation shows that a program has little impact, it nevertheless can provide information on how the program can be improved.
Even though the program does not achieve its official goals, there may be some positive findings that come out of an evaluation about the social problem toward which the program is directed.
In cases where the client ignores the evaluation, there is little, if anything, an evaluator can do to correct the misuse (other than to publish the results in a scholarly journal).

Misuse by the Evaluator

The example just discussed is one type of misuse: the client is politically committed to a program regardless of whether it is producing results, so the evaluation is ignored. It is misuse because the sponsors of the program may have other goals than the official ones (for example, public relations may well be the main goal in the GREAT program) but does not state these underlying goals for various reasons. The evaluator cannot do much about this type of misuse. The other major category of misuse is where the evaluator changes the results in order to satisfy the client. Whatever the motive for doing this (for example, the evaluator is co-opted or the evaluator expects to get additional contracts from the client), the evaluator has control over this type of misuse, and it is therefore a more serious form of misuse. It is difficult to say whether this occurs more often than the first type, but it is certain that there generally will be subtle pressure brought to bear on the evaluator to come up with something positive, particularly if the evaluator's own values support the goals of the program. The following is a case in which I was asked to omit negative findings from the evaluation of an alternative dispute resolution program.

From October 1992 to September 1993, the supreme court of a western state funded seven sites to promote alternative dispute resolution programs in the state. In all of the programs, litigants were encouraged to use mediation instead of judge or jury trials for their small claims and domestic relations suits. Some were in superior courts and others in the justice courts.

Mediation is a process whereby a plaintiff who wants to collect money for an injury, or parties who want a divorce, or someone who wants to collect money owed to him or her, submit their claim to a neutral mediator who tries to get the parties to reach a settlement. The mediator helps the parties reach an agreement but cannot impose an agreement on them. The process is not adversarial, unlike what occurs in a trial before a judge or jury.

Mediation is supposed to save money and time; it saves money for the parties because cases can be heard without lawyers. Also, time is saved if cases can be heard without long delays. It saves money for the state because if enough cases are diverted to mediation, new judges do not have to be appointed, and cases do not need to be heard in a courthouse. In fact, it is preferable to hold them in the community.

The main purpose of the program during the first year was to encourage counties to develop new ways of handling disputes. During the first year, the sites spent time getting their programs started and overcoming implementation obstacles. They organized advisory boards, met with community groups, recruited mediators, provided training, and publicized their programs.

Each of the seven sites is unique; no two developed the same kind of program or handled the same kinds of cases. Some focused strictly on child custody and divorce, whereas others handled only small claims in which lawyers were not involved; some used lawyers as mediators, whereas others used unpaid volunteers; some mandated mediation for some cases, others did not; some were conducted in superior court, and others in the justice courts (lower courts).

Although each was unique, some things were common among all sites that made it likely that the programs would not succeed. The most important was the fact that many lawyers were not very enthusiastic about mediation and the volunteers who were doing the mediations. If lawyers do not tell their clients to use mediation (most people do not know about mediation unless advised by the attorney), the program will not succeed. The evaluation team from ASU (Michael Musheno, a number of graduate students, and I) conducted surveys of lawyers in two of the counties. When asked how much they thought lawyers in their county supported mediation, 42 percent said very little, 42 percent said somewhat, and only 16 percent said very much. Most said it should be used only in a limited number of cases, such as domestic disputes and small civil claims. Moreover, they felt that mediators were not knowledgeable about the law and were not professional. Mediators, on the other hand, felt that lawyers should not be involved in mediation and that they simply recreated the adversarial atmosphere that mediation was supposed to replace. Also, because mediation is supposed to be community-based rather than a part of the formal court system, there was dissatisfaction among some mediators with the fact that mediation was being mandated by the courts in some cases.

Another controversial part of the evaluation pertained to the mediation of child custody and visitation rights in divorce cases. At one site, the mediator claimed a 95 percent success rate. He began his sessions by asking the parties whether domestic violence were being alleged, because if it were, he could not continue the session. Because both the man and woman were present in the same room, there was a power imbalance between the parties in responding to this question. I sat in on one session in which the woman said her husband hit her and threatened to kill her, but she did not want to allege that domestic violence was involved. Moreover, the mediator dealt only with legal custody and visitation rights for children. The more difficult questions of property settlement and child support payments still had to be settled in court by a judge. Thus, the 95 percent success rate was not really accurate in a substantive sense. Also, the evaluation found that very few cases had been mediated during the first year.

When we presented the results to the committee that commissioned the evaluation, one committee member in particular (a judge) objected to the data about the conflict between the lawyers and mediators and about the reference to the fact that only a few cases had been mediated throughout the state. He pressed for revisions in the report. Before describing what we did, I want to put this type of misuse into broader context.

Argument, Persuasion, and the Political Role of Evaluators

That evaluations are political and evaluators are engaged in politics has long been noted by evaluation scholars but ignored by the majority of evaluators (Palumbo, 1987). One of the first to call attention to this was Carol Weiss (1970, 1973) who remarked that although evaluation is a rational enterprise, it takes place in a political context. The three ways politics intrude, according to Weiss (1987), are as follows: the policies and programs with which evaluation deals are the creatures of political decisions; evaluation reports enter the political arena; and by its very nature, evaluation makes implicit political statements about programs. Cronbach and others (1980, p. 67) also pointed out the political nature of evaluation in the following way:

> The evaluator has a political influence even when he does not aspire to it. He can be an arm of those in power, but he loses most of his value in that role if he does not think independently. He can put himself in the service of some partisan interest outside the center of power, but there again his unique contribution is a critical, scholarly habit of mind. He can, we assert, render greatest service if he became an informant to and educator of all parties to a decision, making available to them the lesson of experience and critical thinking. Since information produces power, such diffusion of information is power equalizing.

As Shadish, Cook, and Leviton (1991, p. 351) put it, for Cronbach "the core of social programs and policy is political accommodation among conflicting stakeholders, not rational decision making."

Cronbach's position is somewhat similar to Guba and Lincoln's (1989, p. 203, 250) idea that evaluation should operate in an empowering way, not a disempowering one. They say, "the first step in empowerment, of course, is taken when all stakeholders and others at risk are provided with the opportunity to contribute inputs to the evaluation and have a hand in shaping its focus and its strategies."

Not all evaluation scholars believe that evaluation is political. Berk and Rossi (1977, p. 85) state, "While evaluation research is political, it is no substitute for politics. Social science can demystify, but it remains the task of politics to interpret the meaning of demystification for direction of political policy." Evaluation, in their view, plays a minor role in social change, which occurs only incrementally anyway. Shadish, Cook, and Leviton (1991, p. 385) say that Rossi's position is that "change results from the interplay among interests of these multiple stakeholders, not from evaluation."

Recent developments in epistemology, particularly in social constructionism (Best, 1989, 1993; Kitsuse and Spector, 1973; Miller and Holstein, 1993), do not accept the position that evaluators are independent, objective observers who somehow have an unbiased view of the policies and programs they evaluate. Instead, they are claims makers about the nature, success, or failure of programs. Indeed, evaluation is similar to science in general; it makes claims about the "reality" of social programs.

Some recent evaluation scholars and policy analysts go a step further by proposing that evaluators should participate in the argumentative and persuasive aspects of policy making if they want to have an impact on policy and programs. Fischer and Forester (1993, p. 2) write that policy analysts cannot be objective scientists because they "scan a political environment as much as they locate facts, and they are involved with senses of value even as they identify costs and benefits." Analysts, they go on to say, cannot care only about the internal coherence and quality of their studies, but must be politically astute as well. They do not reject science and its tools, but argue that discourse—the words used in policy analysis—should also be included in this "argumentative turn."

The importance of discourse and of the role of policy analysis and evaluation in this discourse was emphasized in the opening sentence of Majone's (1989) book, *Evidence, Argument, and Persuasion in the Policy Process* as follows: "As politicians know only too well but social scientists too often forget, public policy is made of language. Whether in written or oral form, argument is central in all stages of the policy process." To be effective, evaluators should be involved in this process. Majone (1989, p. 171) notes that "many program evaluations have a narrow managerial focus, being concerned with goal achievement and administrative control rather than with the responsiveness of the program to the divergent values of different individuals and groups." Instead, evaluation should "recognize the legitimacy of the different perspectives" that would "contribute to a shared understanding of the multiple perspectives involved" (Majone, 1989, p. 9).

Thus, in the view of some evaluators, it is important not only to recognize that evaluation is political, but to take part in the discourse that occurs around policies and programs; otherwise, they are not likely to be effective. But does that mean, as Browne and Wildavsky once wrote about the position I took about evaluators being advocates for a wider public interest, that they risk becoming "poor politicians . . . abandoning the concern for error that made them methodologically rigorous and politically neutral" (1984, p. 184)? Fischer and Forester (1993, p. 3) also recognize that although analysts are unavoidably political, they cannot tend only to political factors because they would "quickly sacrifice the substantial integrity of their studies." But how does an evaluator solve the dilemma of becoming a part of the political debate surrounding a program while still maintaining a "scientific" stance? Fischer and Forester say that evaluators must recognize that discourse about policy is crucial in determining policy decisions and an evaluator's scientific tools are a part of the discourse. Hajer (1993) describes how this might be done with regard to the acid rain and air pollution debates in England. In accord with the social constructionist approach, Hajer says that there are many realities in these debates, not just one, and these are created by the language used in various discourse coalitions. The evaluator should focus on this discourse, not on the "facts" of acid rain or air pollution, because there is no reality to the issues; instead, there are only various claims about the reality of acid rain and the evaluator's findings are also a claim whose standings are not necessarily more valued than those of other stakeholders.

Conclusion: The Social Constructionist Solution

If evaluators accept the position that there are multiple competing claims about the nature and effects of a policy or program aimed at a social problem, that evaluators' "scientific" findings are among these various claims, and that the role of evaluators is to recognize the political nature of their role and enter into the political discourse, then the answer to the question posed at the beginning of this article is as follows: it might be a good tactic to drop some of the findings that the client finds objectionable if that enables the evaluator to help promote or further the prospects of the program. This, of course, depends on whether the evaluators believe that the program and its goals are worthwhile and desirable because from this postmodern perspective, evaluators cannot be neutral; they have values that, to be ethical, should not be compromised. It would only be unethical if evaluators made the changes for a program whose goals they believed to be bad social policy. The evaluator is not a neutral technician, but an involved claims maker who has views about the desirability of a program. This does not mean that evaluators should abandon the methodological rigor that provides legitimacy for their involvement (Palumbo, 1987). It simply means that they are more than mere technical experts who serve the interests of managers or decision makers.

The problem posed at the beginning of this chapter pertained to the mediation program evaluation. The committee that commissioned the evaluation wanted the information about the hostile attitudes of the mediators toward lawyers and the lawyers' unfavorable views of the mediators taken out because, they said, this was not really relevant information. They also wanted the information about the relatively few cases that were finally mediated removed because, they said, the evaluation was not supposed to be an impact assessment (although the evaluators believed that most of the members of the committee did not know the difference between impact and process evaluations).

The evaluators agreed to tone down some of the material pertaining to these parts but not remove them completely. This resulted in the evaluation report being accepted by the committee and used in several sites. The director of the program at one of the sites stated to one of the evaluators that the information about the lawyers' opinions about mediation was useful because it made her realize that one of the more important things she had to do was mount a public relations campaign to get the cooperation of the lawyers in the county in order for the program to succeed.

If, as Cronbach believes, the core of social programs and policy is political accommodation among conflicting stakeholders, and if evaluators are one of these stakeholders, then evaluators must sometimes accommodate in order to remain in a discourse coalition and influence the direction of policy and programs. Of course, this does not mean they should be co-opted by program directors, or distort the nature of the evaluation so that it supports a failing program with whose goals they disagree. It certainly does not mean they should do this because they expect to get more contracts from the client. This would indeed be misuse. But it does mean that policy discourse is a matter of give and take. It also means that at times evaluators should realize that some of their findings may be out of place in the particular context. It certainly also means that policy should never be determined solely on the basis of evaluation findings, as once was hoped for by evaluators. As Fischer and Forester (1993) say, it is necessary to demystify technocratic expertise under which analysts operated until quite recently. As a step toward methodological reform, they go on to say, "the contemporary emphasis on arguments and discourse potentially opens the door to a very different kind of epistemological orientation based on a social constructionist conception of knowledge, . . . a dialectic mode of argumentation, and the interpretive methods common to both" (p. 37).

Misuse by an evaluator, therefore, occurs when the reason for changing or revising findings promotes the material self-interests of the evaluator. But it does not occur when the evaluator agrees with the goals of the program and believes that the revisions will increase the chances that the evaluation will be used and will help the program to succeed. On the other hand, misuse does occur when an evaluator acts strictly as a technician and provides a positive evaluation for a program he or she believes has undesirable goals. This is true even if the evaluator does not revise the findings. Thus, misuse of evaluation occurs when an evaluator assumes the role of scientific technician and leaves the value questions to politicians and decision makers.

References

Berk, R. A., and Rossi, P. H. "Doing Good or Worse: Evaluation Research Politically Reexamined." In G. V. Glass (ed.), *Evaluation Studies Review Annual*, vol. 2. Newbury Park, Calif.: Sage, 1977.

Best, J. *Images of Issues*. Hawthorne, N.Y.: Aldine, 1989.

Best, J. "But Seriously Folks: The Limitations of the Strict Constructionist Interpretation of Social Problems." In G. Miller and J. Holstein (eds.), *Constructionist Controversies: Issues in Social Problems and Theory*. Aldine, 1993, pp. 109–131.

Browne, A., and Wildavsky, A. "What Should Evaluation Mean to Implementation." In J. Pressman and A. Wildavsky (eds.), *Implementation* (3rd ed.). Berkeley: University of California Press, 1984.

Cronbach, L. J., and others. *Toward Reform of Program Evaluation*. San Francisco: Jossey-Bass, 1980.

Fischer, F., and Forester, J. (eds.). *The Argumentative Turn in Policy Analysis and Planning*. Durham, N.C.: Duke University Press, 1993.

Guba, E., and Lincoln, Y. *Fourth Generation Evaluation*. Newbury Park, Calif.: Sage, 1989.

Hajer, M. A. "Discourse Coalitions and the Institutionalization of Practice: The Case of Acid Rain in Great Britain." In F. Fischer and J. Forester (eds.), *The Argumentative Turn in Policy Analysis and Planning*. Durham, N.C.: Duke University Press, 1993.

Kitsuse, J. I., and Spector, M. "Toward a Sociology of Social Problems." *Social Problems*, 1973, 20, 407–419.

Majone, G. *Evidence, Argument and Persuasion in the Policy Process*. New Haven, Conn.: Yale University Press, 1989.

Miller, G., and Holstein, J. A. (eds.). *Constructionist Controversies: Issues in Social Problems Theory*. New York: Aldine, 1993.

Palumbo, D. (ed.). *The Politics of Program Evaluation*. Newbury Park, Calif.: Sage, 1987.

Rossi, P. "The Iron Law of Evaluation and Other Metallic Rules." Paper presented at State University of New York, Albany, 1985.

Shadish, W. R., Jr., Cook, T. P., and Leviton, L. C. (eds.). *Foundations of Program Evaluation*. Newbury Park, Calif.: Sage, 1991.

Spergel, I. *Youth Gangs: Problem and Response*. NYGIC Doc. #D0027. Arlington, Va.: National Youth Gang Information Center, 1991.

Weiss, C. H. "The Politicization of Evaluation Research." *Journal of Social Issues*, 1970, 26 (4), 57–68.

Weiss, C. H. "The Politics of Impact Measurement." *Policy Studies Journal*, 1973, 1 (3), 179–183.

Weiss, C. H. "Where Politics and Evaluation Research Meet." In D. J. Palumbo (ed.), *The Politics of Program Evaluation*. Newbury Park, Calif.: Sage, 1987.

DENNIS J. PALUMBO *is regents professor of justice studies at Arizona State University.*

Although there are many advantages of internal evaluation, there are also disadvantages, the most serious of which is potential misuse by managers who want evaluations to appear to objectively support decisions that have already been made.

Use and Abuse of Internal Evaluation

Barbara Poitras Duffy

In his book *Internal Evaluation,* Love (1991) asserts that the accelerated growth of internal evaluation within private, public, and charitable organizations has resulted from a general disenchantment with external evaluators, funding cuts, and the lack of evaluation use. According to House (1986), the shift from external evaluations to internal evaluations has already taken place, representing a major metamorphosis in the field of evaluation research. As a result, many organizations now recognize internal evaluation to be an indispensable tool for their managers and an integral part of the management process.

Internal evaluation has been defined as the process of using staff members who are responsible for evaluating programs or problems of direct relevance to the management of an organization (Love, 1991). The field of internal evaluation draws on a wide variety of methodologies, including the management, systems, and information sciences. It is also a form of action research, frequently focusing on issues of immediate concern to the management of an organization.

Many internal evaluators view themselves as change agents, contributing to the formulation of policy development instead of maintaining the traditional posture of neutrality. Sonnichsen (1988) identifies three critical variables that contribute to the success of internal evaluation offices: location within the organizational structure, staff composition, and operating philosophy. An internal evaluation component that is strategically located within the organizational hierarchy, made up of talented individuals, and functioning within an

The author wishes to thank G. O. Burton and R. C. Sonnichsen for constructive reviews and comments. *Disclaimer:* The opinions expressed in this article do not necessarily reflect those of the FBI.

advocacy role can generate significant organizational change and be acknowledged as an essential organizational element.

Although organizations derive many advantages from the use of internal evaluation, there are also potential disadvantages. Lyon (1989) has suggested that much of the literature addressing internal evaluation has failed to specifically address the roles performed by internal evaluators, focusing instead on the weaknesses of the process that result from both political and survival considerations on the part of the evaluators.

Patton (1986) has provided some insight into the "world of the internal evaluator," highlighting some of the challenges they encounter. These challenges include obtaining participation throughout the evaluation process, dealing with pressure to provide public relations information rather than pure evaluation research, managing additional tasks such as requests for immediate data or reports that detract from their ability to conduct comprehensive evaluations, exclusion from decision-making networks in the development of new initiatives that would benefit from an up-front evaluation perspective, and ensuring the use of evaluation results and recommendations.

This chapter addresses potential misuse of internal evaluation by an organization's executive management when evaluations are commissioned solely to give the appearance of objectively assessing issues, policies, and programs when decisions have already been reached. Furthermore, internal evaluators, as members of these organizations, may be pressured to conduct assessments that by design produce biased findings in order to ensure the outcomes desired by management. A case study is presented based on the experiences of the Federal Bureau of Investigation's (FBI) internal evaluation component, which has been successful in avoiding the abuses that typically arise, due to its organizational placement. Advice to internal evaluators who may find themselves in comparable circumstances is also provided on possible ways to mitigate such abuses.

Internal Evaluation: The Up Side

Internal evaluation can best be described as the process of using members of an organization (who possess the requisite experiences or academic credentials) to assess their organization's policies, programs, or problems and report their findings and recommendations to the head of the organization. To date, numerous books and articles have been written about the advantages of internal evaluation components. Perhaps one of the greatest benefits to an organization with an internal evaluation function is a product of the organizational membership of its evaluators.

This membership helps to ensure cost-effective and high-quality evaluations in three principal ways: as a member of the organization, an internal evaluator is in the best position to develop an evaluation strategy that is best suited to the nature of the organization; this membership ensures a long-term organizational commitment; and membership further affords the internal evaluator knowledge of the organization's culture, as well as access to insider information concerning the issues, policies, programs, and relationships under examination. Organizational membership also provides the internal evaluator with knowledge of the perceptions and priorities that exist at various levels throughout an organization, and also helps to facilitate client involvement in the evaluative process.

Finally, the development of an optimal evaluation strategy is key to ensuring the use of study findings. Because the expectations of employees are often raised during the evaluation process, the credibility of internal evaluators is enhanced when decisions are made and changes occur as a result of their efforts. In the long run, this membership strengthens the organizational credibility of an internal evaluation component.

Internal Evaluation: The Down Side

There are several potential disadvantages to an organization's reliance on internal evaluation components. These disadvantages include the need for the occasional outside perspective, the lack of cost-effectiveness in maintaining individuals on the payroll who possess highly specialized skills that may only be needed occasionally, and the need for credibility with and accountability to various oversight groups such as Congress. To date, much of the literature written about the inherent weaknesses of internal evaluation has focused on the potential for conflicting agendas within an organization's components and the potential threat to the careers of internal evaluators, which may ultimately constrain their research efforts.

It has been further suggested that the credibility of internal evaluators may be suspect; there is a perception that these evaluators will consciously (or subconsciously) embrace the positions of executive managers, leading to weak methodologies and biased results. Kennedy (1983) asserts that in some instances, the dynamics of an organization can be so overwhelming that in order to survive, internal evaluators may be forced to adapt their roles to the needs of the organization or manipulate the organization so that it will accept the role that the evaluators believe to be most appropriate. Furthermore, although these adaptive strategies may ultimately result in support for evaluation findings, they simultaneously diminish the professional standards of the evaluator.

In addition, the organizational pressures imposed on internal evaluators can be significant. These individuals may find themselves being drawn into the political decision-making process by virtue of appearing to conduct an evaluation that executive management has requested. Their credibility and balanced perspective may be hurt by continuous conflicts over policies and programs. As House (1986) observes, internal evaluators may find themselves used as a tool of the administration, being pressured to produce information to support decisions that have already been made. This pressure can be blatant or subtle, but if successful, will have serious consequences for the internal evaluation function by resulting in the misuse of the evaluation research.

Furthermore, some of the challenges experienced by internal evaluators ultimately affect the credibility of their role, as their study findings and credibility are integral to the use of these findings (Lyon, 1989). As mentioned earlier, the organization's expectations for change are elevated during the course of any evaluative effort. When nothing happens following an evaluation, the internal evaluator's credibility is seriously diminished and the next time he or she attempts to elicit cooperation from the rest of the organization on another project, it will be met with skepticism.

Finally, the ethical dilemmas that confront internal evaluators are not to be taken lightly. Adams (1985) believes that these challenges include pressure to identify and emphasize positive findings, avoid conducting evaluations that challenge basic organizational tenets or have the potential to result in negative findings, provide "ritual functions" rather than encourage management to use the results of an evaluation, and potentially misuse access to privileged information and sources.

Internal Evaluation Within the FBI

Internal evaluation has been described as a powerful organizational intervention, and its methodology depends on political and practical constraints (Love, 1991). Within the FBI, internal evaluations are conducted by the Office of Planning and Evaluation (OPE), which has had primary responsibility for conducting internal program and policy reviews through management studies since 1972. OPE is charged with coordinating bureauwide planning, promoting research and development, evaluating plans and policies, and conducting surveys and studies. OPE conducts evaluations to assist executive management with the administration, organization, and operational aspects of the FBI, and is staffed by both civilian and sworn law enforcement personnel.

The FBI's internal evaluators are used in three principal ways: as formative evaluators, reviewing major investigative and administrative programs; as policy analysts, studying topics selected by top management with a short response time; and as management consultants, reviewing specific management problems (Sonnichsen, 1988). These reviews are an important management tool as the FBI seeks to maximize the efficiency and effectiveness of operations of its fifty-six field divisions and headquarters components during a period of severe budgetary and personnel reductions. Key to its success in having an impact is its placement within the organization, as OPE is a centralized unit that reports directly to the head of the agency (Sonnichsen, 1988).

Depending on the nature of the evaluation, a variety of methodologies are used by OPE, including qualitative strategies. Over the past five years, OPE has used focus group interviews extensively, finding them to be a valuable tool for its internal evaluators, especially in an environment where credibility is key to achieving employee cooperation (Duffy, 1993). Although all affected parties are afforded updates, briefings, and report drafts so as to provide them with an opportunity to comment on its findings, OPE has direct access to the director of the FBI with respect to problem identification and the presentation of findings and recommendations. Because the ultimate objective of OPE is program improvement, reports are written for internal use only. There is no public relations use of its work products.

Case Study: 1990 Assessment on the Locations of FBI Field Offices

Before 1987, the FBI had never conducted a comprehensive assessment of the locations of its field offices. However, during a routine inspection of the Butte, Montana division, the director asked the FBI's Office of Inspections to assess the viability of relocating the headquarters (or management oversight) of this division to either Boise, Idaho, or Salt Lake City, Utah. Based on the findings of the inspection, it was determined that a consolidation of the Butte division with the Salt Lake City division was viable. As a result, the attorney general was notified of an FBI proposal to consolidate the Butte and Salt Lake City field divisions.

Unfortunately, this proposal was met with tremendous resistance, both internally and externally. In an attempt to disrupt this action, a senator from Montana blocked the ongoing confirmation hearings of former FBI director William H. Webster for his future role as director of the Central Intelligence Agency. In order to release Webster from this predicament, a compromise was reached with the senator wherein OPE would conduct a comprehensive assessment of this issue following the appointment of William S. Sessions as director of the FBI. Based on this assessment, OPE recommended the consolidation of these two divisions during a briefing to the director and executive management. Later that year, the director announced that this consolidation was approved.

In July 1988, OPE conducted a second assessment that addressed a proposal made by the head of the Atlanta division to consolidate the Savannah and Atlanta divisions. Based on the findings of this evaluation, OPE identified an opportunity to consolidate two more FBI field divisions. Acting on the recommendation of OPE, the director announced that these divisions would also be consolidated in December 1989.

In the fall of 1990, OPE was again asked by a high-ranking FBI official at headquarters to conduct an evaluation of the feasibility and merits of realigning the territories of two other FBI field offices. His request was ostensibly predicated on the need to more evenly distribute the operational and liaison responsibilities for five states across the two affected field offices. As a result, the overall objective of this evaluation was to determine whether the mission of the FBI in one region of the country would be most effectively served by maintaining the previously established territorial alignments. The evaluation included an examination of the managerial span of control of the special agents in charge, the probable impact of realignment on the FBI's investigative mission, a cost–benefit analysis, and a review of other key logistical issues. Interviews were conducted with affected representatives of federal, state, and local law enforcement agencies, as well as FBI personnel.

During the scoping phase of this study, it became apparent that the official who had requested this study was already predisposed to realigning the territories of these two field offices and he expressed his preference throughout the organization and to the evaluation staff. He was advised that OPE would remain objective during the course of its assessment, keep affected parties advised as to the study's progress, and report its findings to the director of the FBI.

After collecting preliminary information from the appropriate oversight components at FBI Headquarters, OPE conducted a site visit to Division A, which stood to benefit from the proposed realignment. By the time the OPE evaluators arrived at this division, nearly all of the people who were scheduled to be interviewed about the proposed realignment appeared to have been thoroughly briefed so as to espouse, rather articulately, the party-line position that favored the change. In fact, individuals who would not normally have certain knowledge or be in a position to comment in any detail about the operational aspects of the proposed realignment, such as representatives from local law enforcement agencies (who were not FBI employees), and members of the FBI's clerical staff, were able to concisely explain all of the perceived advantages that would result from the realignment.

Though initially amusing, it quickly became annoying as the management of this office, in coaching its employees before the arrival of the evaluation staff, made it difficult for the evaluators to collect the information they needed. However, once the evaluation team confronted the management of Division A, stating that they were aware of what had occurred and that it would be unsuccessful in skewing the outcome of this evaluation, the team was able to obtain the information it needed to conduct an accurate review. Predictably, confronting these managers about the evaluation team's perceptions of what had occurred to prepare employees for the team's arrival was uncomfortable. As it turned out, ten years earlier, one of the field managers had supervised a member of the evaluation team and had mistakenly believed that he could exert some influence over the evaluator.

The following week, OPE conducted a second site visit to Division B, which stood to lose territory under the proposed realignment. However, by the time the OPE staffers arrived in this division, the employees of Division A convinced those of Division B that the evaluation team supported the realignment. As a result, the evaluators were met with a great deal of hostility and mistrust by the employees of Division B. In order to overcome the visible animosity and regain their credibility, the evaluators modified their plans to conduct only a limited number of focus group interview sessions and increased the number of sessions so as to include all of the stakeholders of the division to afford them an opportunity to contribute to the evaluative process.

Briefly, a focus group is a small group interview where eight to twelve individuals are encouraged to interact and share information on a specific topic. Whenever appropriate, OPE evaluators conduct multiple focus group sessions with FBI employees during the course of their assessments. Because the FBI is a closed, tightly knit community, what ensures the success of this strategy is the credibility of the evaluators, who as internal evaluators and fellow members of the organization understand the policies, practices, and politics of the FBI (Duffy, 1993).

Although it has been suggested that it may be preferable to use participants who do not know each other (Krueger, 1988), this is not always possible nor desirable when conducting focus groups within the FBI. Although it is a large organization, it is difficult to select a group of individuals within a division who do not know each other, especially if they have been assigned there for some time. In fact, the presence of an individual who is not known to others in these focus group sessions has been found to have an inhibiting effect on the other participants, as the desire for continued confidentiality once the session disbands cannot be ensured.

In this particular situation, the OPE team ran multiple focus group interview sessions, stratified by employee position, rank, and program assignment (such as drugs or white-collar crime). This approach successfully mitigated the concerns of the employees of Division B that the OPE evaluators were predisposed to produce the outcome desired by the requesting official. Because they were included in the evaluation process, these employees ultimately let down their defenses and cooperated with the evaluators by providing objective information to make informed decisions about the realignment proposal.

Based on the qualitative information collected during the site visits and a review of the quantitative data provided by the program managers at FBI Headquarters, the evaluation team concluded that the FBI's mission would be most effectively served by maintaining the current configuration of the two field divisions, despite the desires of the requesting official. This recommendation was forwarded to and ultimately approved by the director.

Lessons Learned

Several factors came together to help the evaluation team overcome the potential for misuse of the internal evaluation by the requesting official, ultimately preserving its credibility. The first factor that contributed to a positive outcome was the organizational membership of the evaluation team, which afforded them insider knowledge into the politics of the situation. Because the FBI is a closed community with a strong organizational culture, an internal evaluation component made up of members of the organization is imperative to achieving meaningful cooperation during the course of any evaluation effort.

Second, positioning in the organizational hierarchy is also important to avoid these abuses. In this instance, the organizational location of the evaluation component insulated the evaluation team from any negative repercussions as a result of their evaluation findings, helping to ensure the integrity of the evaluators and their findings. Internal evaluation components must have direct access to their director or a comparable senior official in order to obtain approval for study recommendations, which in turn reduces parochialism and minimizes individual bias.

The third factor that helped to prevent an abuse of the internal evaluation function was the methodology used by the evaluation team. The heavy reliance on the focus group interview technique in effect publicized the key study issues by addressing them in a forum where the stakeholders themselves would familiarize themselves with the advantages and disadvantages of the realignment proposal. This reassured the stakeholders that all relevant issues were being addressed, not just those of the study's requesting official.

Although other internal evaluation components may not always have the luxury of determining their organizational location or chain of command so as to ensure direct access to the head of their organization, they do benefit from the strengths associated with organizational membership. Furthermore, by promoting openness surrounding the issues under consideration, the evaluation methodology used by internal evaluators can help to mitigate potential abuses on the part of managers who commission studies. Use of the focus group interview technique goes a long way in helping to achieve buy-in from stakeholders, as well as publicizing all of the relevant issues in an open forum.

References

Adams, K. "Gamesmanship for Internal Evaluators: Knowing When to 'Hold 'Em' and When to 'Fold 'Em.'" *Evaluation and Program Planning,* 1985, 8, 53–57.
Duffy, B. P. "Focus Groups: An Important Research Technique for Internal Evaluation Units." *Evaluation Practice,* 1993, 14 (2), 133–139.
House, E. R. "Internal Evaluation." *Evaluation Practice,* 1986, 7, 63–64.
Kennedy, M. "The Role of the In-House Evaluator." *Evaluation Review,* 1983, 7, 519–541.
Krueger, R. A. *Focus Groups: A Practical Guide for Applied Research.* Newbury Park, Calif.: Sage, 1988.
Love, A. *Internal Evaluation: Building Organizations from Within.* Newbury Park, Calif.: Sage, 1991.
Lyon, E. "In-House Research: A Consideration of Roles and Advantages." *Evaluation and Program Planning,* 1989, 12, 241–248.
Patton, M. Q. *Utilization-Focused Evaluation.* Newbury Park, Calif.: Sage, 1986.
Sonnichsen, R. C. "Advocacy Evaluation: A Model for Internal Evaluation Offices." *Evaluation and Program Planning,* 1988, 11, 141–148.

BARBARA POITRAS DUFFY is a management analyst assigned to the Office of Planning and Evaluation, Inspection Division, Federal Bureau of Investigation.

Politicization and a fiscal control emphasis in a state government agency paralyzed the operation of a previously functional and well-staffed evaluation division, as described in this case study.

The Gradual Extinction of Evaluation Within a Government Agency

Carol T. Mowbray

The evaluation literature reflects three assumptions concerning the growth, impact, and appropriate use of evaluation activities: positive outcomes depend on the behavior of the evaluators themselves, use or misuse of evaluations reflects the characteristics of the decision makers, and problems in evaluation are resource-related. The first two assumptions have been explored thoroughly (perhaps ad nauseam) in the past. Factors reflecting evaluators' behavior include timeliness in report production; reports that are too technical, too jargon-laden, too long, or too hard to understand; communication formats that are not audience-friendly (with executive summaries, simple and attractive graphics, and verbal briefings); and poor-quality studies with inadequate methodologies, sampling, reliability, or validity (Ginsburg, 1992; Mangano, 1992; Mowbray, 1988; Preskill, 1991). Evaluators have also been faulted for their inability to operate within the political environment; to understand what decision makers really need to know, for what purpose, and within what timelines; and to practice behaviors that are appropriate outside academia, such as selecting topics of interest to policy makers, planning for report completion to coincide with significant dates in the budget or policy-making process, and producing practical and usable recommendations (Grob, 1992; Richardson, 1992).

There is an equally familiar literature that attributes evaluation's problems to decision makers: they do not know what they really want, they do not have the proper training to support and use evaluations, their personal information and biases compete with evaluation-based results, and so on (Mowbray, 1988; Preskill, 1991).

NEW DIRECTIONS FOR PROGRAM EVALUATION, no. 64, Winter 1994   © Jossey-Bass Publishers

The third set of reasons posited as relevant to evaluation's impact concerns resources: the amount of time, money, and expertise allotted to evaluation activities, including the training and experience of evaluation staff, internal versus external evaluators, and funding availability. It also includes evaluation support: identification of stakeholders, involvement of stakeholders early in the development of the evaluation's purpose and design, and investment of stakeholders in the quality and utility of the results. Resource deficiencies may occur for a variety of reasons: evaluators' failings (such as lack of planning and design cost overruns), management problems (such as hiring or contracting out to poorly qualified evaluators and failing to follow through on resource commitments), or external circumstances (such as economic cutbacks or budget shortfalls wherein research, evaluation, and training are seen as superfluous in comparison with maintaining budget and finance or core services). For example, at the federal level, evaluation spending decreased 37 percent from 1980 to 1988, with staffing levels down 22 percent (Havens, 1992) as administrators made decisions about which types of federal activities to cut in order to meet reduced budget targets. However, in contrast to evaluation cutbacks, government functions such as auditing and compliance reviews actually enjoyed funding expansions (Moran, 1990).

Recent writings concerning the use or misuse of evaluation suggest that factors related to organizational context may have major impacts, which as yet have been underestimated and infrequently researched. Preskill (1991) discusses the effects of the culture of the institution—its history, political climate, beliefs, and value systems—on evaluation. Newman, Smukler, Griffin, and Fishman (1992) identified "authoritative initiative" as one of seven loci influencing the impact of state-level evaluation. This variable reflects the clarity of an evaluation mandate (by statute or administrative rules) vis à vis authority, responsibility, and resources.

Others have identified highly politicized environments and strong ideological positions as significant for the use, misuse, or even existence of an evaluation enterprise. When, because of entrenched political positions, executives already "know" which programs work and which do not, there is no need to study them; when executives are focused only on the possible political repercussions of objective reports that document program implementation problems, inefficiencies, or lack of impact, they have no interest in supporting such studies. Chelimsky (in Wye and Sonnichsen, 1992) has attributed evaluation reductions during the Reagan administration to such factors: "It seems very likely to me that evaluation findings will continue to fall on deaf ears when ideological requirements or constraints are so strong—or an administration's investment in an area is so great—that neutral information is not even sought. In those cases, policymakers and managers are simply too committed to decisions already taken to be able to use new research results" (p. 187).

Wye and Sonnichsen (1992) note that during the same time period, government concerns switched from program effectiveness to control of financial operations "to protect against unwanted intruders who may waste resources and embarrass incumbents" (p. 194). As control functions in agencies increased, evaluation functions decreased. Chelimsky (1992) indicates that federal reductions in evaluation resources have also distorted findings.

This chapter presents a case study concerning how politicization of the overall operation of a state agency paralyzed a robust evaluation unit and eventually led to its demise. The growth and development of the unit in the mid-1970s and the agency's supportive climate are first described. Next, information is presented on how a gubernatorial change and appointment of a new agency director produced an environment where rational decision-making processes were obscured by the need to assuage political friends and foes. In the resulting organizational culture, budgetary control issues dominated and programmatic concerns dwindled. Finally, the impact of this politicized and financially fixated environment on its evaluation functions (namely, interference with activities through extensive bureaucratic review, slowdowns in processing paperwork, increased compliance requirements, and additional criteria for approvals) is presented. The discussion section explores the implications of this case study for the future of internal evaluators in government operations and suggests alternative strategies to counteract misuse and mistreatment of evaluation functions. (The name of the department in this case study has been altered to depersonalize the events described and to broaden their generalizability to other content areas. The department was responsible for some aspects of health, education, and social services to an identified population. The author was directly involved in the case as the director of the division.)

Background

In the mid 1970s, a state-level Department of Human Services (DHS) established a separate organizational unit responsible for evaluation functions during the second term of a stable gubernatorial reign that was to span fourteen years. The role identified for evaluation in the department was based on a rational model of planning and program development. That is, a needs assessment identifies the type and extent of need and a demonstration program is developed to meet these needs. Program evaluation then examines effectiveness and the need for program revisions or further needs assessment and planning. Once a demonstration project model has been proven effective, it can then be disseminated and replicated in other locations—again, with evaluation components in place to identify needed modifications for the new sites. The staff of the evaluation bureau were primarily young professionals with masters and doctoral level training in applied research and evaluation. From a beginning staff of four, the bureau increased over the next eight years to a staff of thirty. The bureau also had grant money available to fund demonstration projects with evaluation components and to competitively solicit external (mainly university-based) researchers and evaluators to conduct targeted studies through a request-for-proposals process. The bureau staff conducted evaluations of existing and new demonstration projects themselves and in collaboration with university staff, developed proposal requests, monitored external evaluation contractors, and wrote applications for external funds. At its height, the bureau's budget was approximately $7 million. Its evaluation products had been used consistently (for example, to obtain replication funding for programs and to initiate policy changes through a Governor's Interdepartmental Task Force). In terms of external authorizations, the necessity of an evaluation function was identified in the department's code, but specific funding levels, products, or activities were never statutorily mandated.

Political and Organizational Change

In the 1980s, the long-time incumbent governor was replaced in a hotly contested and close election that also resulted in a turnover in party control. With a switch in administrations came changes in DHS operations, which eventually had profound effects on its evaluation staffing, organization, and resources. After the election, it was immediately obvious that most gubernatorial actions were politically motivated, to promote either the party's agenda or the new governor's political future. However, for several years, there was relative calm in DHS because the governor had continued the appointment of a senior state-level executive with bipartisan affiliations as the department's director. This calm may have been misleading, though, as it was accompanied by an obvious reluctance to address needed policy and practice reforms. The early effect of the new administration on operations was to produce a feeling of malaise.

However, late in the governor's first term, scandal surrounding the department broke out concerning alleged sexual abuse of service recipients and staffing negligence leading to violent behaviors, injury, and death. These incidents received widespread press coverage and produced several costly lawsuits. The appointment of a new DHS director followed. The new director was young and relatively inexperienced in human services administration. He had no executive experience in state government, but strong party political ties.

Although the new director was not experienced in management, decision making, or leadership, he was experienced in the political game. The governor had gone through significant battles and costs early in his first administration to get a tax increase approved and had won a somewhat close reelection. The last thing he wanted to see was more controversy in DHS. The new director set out to ensure that calm prevailed. One way to do this was to appease key legislators, as well as important constituents and advocates who were known to "take to the press." These individuals often came to the director with requests. Mostly, these involved funding small projects or intervening on behalf of a recipient to get him or her into or out of a program. In prior administrations, these requests were mostly defused—the usual strategy was to cite budget deficits, refer them to the relevant agency director with an explanation about local authority, or refer them to Central Office program administrators with an explanation about requirements under statute, policy, or administrative procedure that precluded any direct action on the request. These stalls or diffusion techniques usually seemed to be accepted by the requesters. However, during the new director's tenure, they were used less and less.

Direct requests for project funding were frequently granted. The demonstration and evaluation approach, with its equitable procedures to solicit and select funding recipients and stringent requirements for documentation and outcome effectiveness measurements, was abandoned, except for existing projects. Instead, unsolicited proposals from special interest groups were readily approved (often with minimal internal review), and funds were made available with no attempt to include evaluation requirements.

However, granting of special funding requests was bounded. There was only a certain amount of slack in a budget made up primarily of line-item expenditures. Although these requests were necessarily bounded by external reality, requests for special treatment or privileges for individual service recipients were not. When such requests emerged during the new directorship, they appeared to have been granted to a much greater extent than they had been in the past. Such requests for favors are stimulated by positive reinforcement. Word spreads readily, causing a snowball effect. Saying "yes" to requests for special treatment created a proliferation of such requests. Departmental leadership did not see any need to respond positively only to "important" requesters, or perhaps they lacked the capacity to make these distinctions. Questions were initially asked about the significance of any requester, but this screen soon passed beyond "who they knew" to "who they *might* know." As an example, a letter for the director's signature to an errant contractor, terminating funding for an evaluation project, was followed one or two days later by a call from the director. His first question was not, "Do you have sufficient documentation of nonperformance to cancel the contract?" but rather, "Is this guy connected?"

The level of effort required to produce special interventions on behalf of individual cases should not be underestimated. Pushing buttons to produce action outside of the usual chain of command and beyond the status quo is not an easy task in a large governmental bureaucracy. This often requires expertise as to whose buttons to push or where requests would be most easily accommodated. Nor can the exception process be delegated to secretaries or junior analysts. Calling up an agency director and telling him or her to make exceptions to eligibility criteria, payment requirements, admission priorities, or other established procedures must be done by a state bureaucrat of equal or higher standing. DHS bureau directors were given more and more special exceptions to handle and soon were spending most of their time on high-level case management.

The granting of special intervention requests is not without costs in terms of effects on field staff, either. Frequently telling program administrators to act outside of normal operating procedures and reversing their decisions causes them to lose credibility with their staffs and erodes their confidence and autonomy of action. Thus, program administrators in the field began to evince a paralysis of action. If questions or situations arose that could be viewed as controversial, they were more and more reluctant to make decisions or take actions themselves: "Better ask Central Office" became the characteristic watchwords. Now bureau directors were kept busy not just in passing down directives from above, but in transmitting questions from below, which in turn generated more directives from above. It was soon the case that the director had to decide everything (even trivial matters) and had to sign everything (even routine letters that should have come from staff).

As can be easily imagined, with all this transmitting and directing, directing and transmitting, neither the bureau directors nor the deputy director or director had any time to do what they were supposed to do: provide leadership and make decisions on important issues of planning, policy, and procedures. In most bureaucracies, when direction from the top is absent, some force usually moves in to fill the void. In this case, it was budget and finance.

When he started, the new director raised the status of the Budget Office. Having little experience in administration, but having lots of experience observing the political process, he knew that ignorance about fiscal issues was the easiest way to look foolish before the legislature. It was crucial that the inexperienced director have a budget director he could rely on to prepare budgets, provide informed answers in budget hearings, write responses for his signature regarding budget questions, and help locate money for special projects. Furthermore, with a nonsupportive budget director, he could easily be stabbed in the back. Thus, not only was the budget director relied on closely, she was also rewarded by having her requests granted and her suggestions followed. The budget director's motivation toward power and control complemented this expanded role.

With an absence of programmatic leadership, directives and dictates for priorities, plans, and new projects emanated more and more from the budget and finance area. All this fit very well with the overriding goal of avoiding political controversy—what better saber to rattle than the possibility of an audit exception? Such a threat could truly strike terror in any bureaucrat whose prime directive was to avoid making waves and to keep up good appearances (Garvey, 1993). Indeed, the possibility of fiscal problems and of audit exceptions was not foreign to the department. There had already been significant revenue losses from retrospective federal audits. Beginning with budget cutbacks in the early 1980s, the department became significantly dependent on federal revenues for services. Loss of these through audit exceptions would have created major operating deficits. Thus, there were many reasons why fiscal issues were important.

As the power and control of budget and finance increased, their scope of influence expanded to affect not just what emanated from the executive office, but also what went into the executive office. This was done by instituting a review process for almost everything the director signed: policy documents, contracts, even no-cost contract extensions. Grant applications for outside funds were not exempt from this extensive review process, even where the funding required no match and no resource commitments. The list of reviewers took up an entire signature page: the supervisor, the bureau director, the chief accountant, the finance director, the administrative services bureau director, the deputy director, the budget director, and then (if it made it that far) the director. Exacerbating the problem of this long list of reviewers, there were no parameters established for any of their reviews: anybody could hold up the process because of anything he or she did not like.

Within four years, the budget and finance offices had established full power and control. Politicization of decision making had resulted in bureau directors spending all their time implementing special requests and transmitting questions and problems up for decision making to the director because of a self-protection mentality and paralysis of action from field program administrators. Budget and financial operations stepped in to fill the void in leadership and decision making, initiating policy and procedure directives, directing planning initiatives, and halting any input to the director that may have presented contrary points of view or competition for power and authority.

What Happened to Evaluation?

In two years, the following outcomes resulted for the evaluation division: endless paperwork, delays in contract signatures, delays and threatened disapproval of new grant applications, interference with federally funded projects, and expanded administrative oversight and control.

Endless paperwork was generated in response to memos from finance and accounting, many of which were written seemingly at the whim of an individual staff member and questioned established approval procedures. For example, for many years the standing committee reviewing human subject issues in research and evaluation proposals (which the division staffed) held alternate monthly meetings via telephone conference calls to reduce travel time for members and costs to the department. One month, the bill for the conference phone call was denied payment. A memo duplicating much of the information already on the telephone bill was required before payment was made.

Often, it appeared as though what bureaucrats perceived as the weakest links were singled out for financial scrutiny. For example, members of special population committees (such as the Women's Committee) that the division worked with to develop program and evaluation proposals had requests for reimbursements related to making presentations on behalf of the committee denied because finance determined this was an inappropriate reimbursable expense for a committee member, despite approvals from division and bureau directors. Another example: a division employee who was blind, whose friends or babysitter drove her in her own car on short travel assignments, had her requests for mileage reimbursements suddenly denied, although they had been routinely approved for several years and had all her supervisors' signatures. Using their own criteria, finance determined that if she needed a driver, she should request the establishment of a position to fill this function, and then that individual could be reimbursed for mileage. Of course, because there was a hiring freeze and no funds available to fill vacancies, this was just another Catch-22 stall. Although some scrutiny was borne by all units, attention to staff activity in evaluation and demonstration projects seemed to be higher. This may have been because of the perceived peripheral status of these areas; perhaps because the nature of the work required more exceptions to normal practices and involved more diverse individuals with specialized skills and needs; or because "a special project is exposed to the hostile scrutiny of those who feel left out" (Garvey, 1993, p. 154).

Delays in contract signatures were a frequent occurrence, including projects that were 100 percent federally funded. Most often, the delays occurred in the budget office and were attributed to a variety of usually irrelevant causes: the contracts were misplaced, inexplicably sent to another party who claimed to have never received them, delayed because of current budget problems, deferred until a current fiscal crisis was resolved, or questioned because of possible duplication. Many delays could be predicted because of particular biases obvious in budget or finance toward a particular contractor (for example, a specific university) or a particular contract area (for example, battered women). As an example, proposals received in response to a competitive request for proposals for homeless demonstration projects were reviewed and recommended for funding in priority order by an objective committee of experts. All the contracts resulting from these recommendations were processed and passed on to the director for signature, except one from the budget director's least favorite county. This proposal (which the committee had ranked number one) was not signed until two months later. This was due to an endless series of questions about the service appropriateness and duplication raised by the budget director—questions the review committee had already considered in detail and with substantially more expertise than she had.

A contract with a state university to carry out research activities funded totally from a federal grant was delayed from September until December in 1988, causing financial problems for the research assistant who was to be paid under this grant. A service demonstration project suffered the same fate. Contracts for federally funded projects at two local agencies were submitted in early September and not signed until December. In fact, signature at that date was obtained under pressure due to the arrival of federal site visitors and the need to have the contract issue resolved before their visit. This time, the refusal of the budget office to approve the contracts was accompanied by a flurry of questions and memos back and forth; most of the responses were summaries of previous correspondence, produced to answer the same questions six or more months earlier. These contracts were near duplications of ones that had been approved by the budget office and signed by the director the year before as merely continuation funding for the same project. The fact that the project was entirely federally funded and that these delays could seriously affect receipt of federal funds did not facilitate a timely review, nor did arguments about the effect on staff and the quality of their service delivery, knowing that without a contract their employment tenure was in jeopardy.

Delays and threatened disapproval of new grant applications were also experienced. Although the director expressed a priority on increased outside funding, the list of signatures required in the review process for grant applications was nearly as long as the applications themselves. This was true even when program and evaluation staff had collaborated on the development and the director had given prior approval to submission plans. Not only was the number of reviewers excessive, but there were no parameters established for their review. Anyone could object to anything they did not like, even if it was totally out of their area of responsibility or expertise. On one occasion, the chief accountant refused to sign his approval for a grant application developed collaboratively with a university because their indirect rate was, in his opinion, too high. His solution was to find another university as a subcontractor. It did not matter to him that this was a federally approved rate, modest compared to some universities, or that university faculty had written half the grant application. On another occasion, the budget office refused to approve a grant application that required an evaluation component because it specified the researcher and the university who would be the contractor; the civil service and management and budget offices had never objected to this common practice in the past. The budget director's only reply was refusal because she did not believe that it was good practice.

Departments outside the evaluation division interfered with federally funded projects. Besides refusing to sign contracts in a timely fashion, there was also more direct interference in the implementation of grants, in terms of staffing requirements. On one research demonstration project, the department's hiring freeze committee refused to authorize refilling a secretarial vacancy, although it was 100 percent federally funded. The rationale was that the department was in the midst of a secretarial study that should be completed before any new secretaries were hired; the position of an existing secretary might be abolished as a result of the study, and vacant positions should be held open in the event that this happened. Although this rationale was offered, the maneuver hinted an attempt to supplant state funds with federal (which is strictly disallowed by federal funding authorities). However, before the study's results were implemented, a state hiring freeze was imposed and the department claimed that it could not get an exception. At that point, approval was given to hire a contract temporary from an outside secretarial service. When this paperwork was finally approved, there was a freeze on all contract personnel employment. Every solution was rebuffed, rejected, reviewed, and revised. After a year and a half of no secretarial services, the money was redirected to other parts of the project. It was not a very efficient solution because project administrators wound up doing their own secretarial work, but it did free up money to do more research.

The most notable example of financial interference occurred at the beginning of a research demonstration project that had been submitted for federal funding, competitively reviewed, and approved. In the budget for the project, the evaluation specialist position was set up to be temporary civil service (for the three-year project duration) at the insistence of budget and finance. Shortly after funding notification, a request to establish this position was submitted and deferred. More information was submitted; more deferrals occurred. Finally, three months later, the Hiring Freeze Committee denied the request. The rationale was that the evaluation division already had enough staff. The committee doubted whether they were all fully used and thought that one of them should take on this assignment (and consequently have their salary charged to the federal grant). Memos and documentation produced to refute this claim and to indicate that the practice suggested would be supplanting state funds with federal were all ignored. A specific staff person was identified to do the job. The division director suggested that federal officials should be contacted and asked whether this change from what was promised in the grant application (a new position as an enhancement of state research and evaluation activities) was allowable. A directive was issued not to do so because the answer would obviously be no. The staff person ordered to take on this new position felt that the assignment was inappropriate. He hired an attorney, who communicated with the federal project officer, who eventually communicated with the department, much to their dismay. Of course, the federal official indicated what the department knew and did not want to ask: that this practice was not allowable.

Expanded administrative oversight and control made it difficult for the evaluation division to carry out routine activities. The administrator of the evaluation division bore most of the brunt of these conflicts with DHS officials. In the previous example, the division director was chastised for not having locked files so that the employee in question was able to access internal correspondence and copy it for his attorney. Another incident involved a sensitive investigation of service recipients' deaths, which was in progress. The director's own advisory council requested evaluation staff to present interim findings and a report was given, on the assumption that the director would have approved this item being on his own council's agenda. A bureau director had been briefed on an ongoing basis concerning the results, but had seen no cause for alarm. In contrast, the council members and the public in attendance were outraged. A flurry of bad publicity and attempts to quell the furor followed. Evaluation staff were reprimanded for not following appropriate chain of command procedures for making presentations and directed to develop boilerplate language prohibiting contractors from presenting research results without prior written DHS approval or a sixty-day review period.

The Demise of the Evaluation Division

The evaluation division staff did not respond well to the controversies, cutbacks, and restrictions they were experiencing. Although state funds had been reduced (diverted to special funding requests), federal funding sources were still available. However, pursuing any type of action—proposing an evaluation study, submitting a grant application, getting contracts signed to spend federal funds, staffing committees to carry out assigned functions, or disseminating and presenting study results—produced such a level of conflict and paperwork as to all but eliminate the time and energy to do anything. As Garvey (1993) points out, "a web of controls" can demoralize and breed discouragement. After a year or so of these experiences, staff vacancies began occurring, with early retirements and transfers to other bureaus and departments. Of course, no approvals were received to fill state-funded vacancies. A second factor in the reduction of the division's staffing was that existing federally funded projects ended, as inevitably occurs. However, for numerous reasons, sufficient new federal funds were not received to provide replacement staffing: there were fewer state-funded staff to write grant applications, the internal review process for the applications had become more and more cumbersome, and fewer submitted applications were funded, perhaps due to lack of quality, reflecting staff resources committed to producing the applications, or perhaps because the state's declining reputation in program development and evaluation and in administering grant funds preceded it.

Because of the greater paperwork requirements and administrative oversight, existing staff spent a greater percentage of their time writing memos and justifying expenditures. There were also increased inquiries from auditors, budget, and finance staff concerning prior federally funded projects. Unfortunately, positions funded under these projects had terminated and staff had left for other jobs, making it even more burdensome for those remaining to produce information to answer more and more detailed criticisms, questions, and allegations about funding exceptions. The director of the evaluation division spent an increasing proportion of time attempting to get these procedures simplified, as well as trying to support staff. Gradually, although an evaluation function theoretically still existed, because of resource limitations, meaningful evaluation activity was all but eliminated.

In disgust and dismay, the director finally left for an academic opportunity. Some of the division's staff were reassigned to the program bureaus, supposedly to make evaluation more accessible to them. For the staff that remained, evaluation and demonstration project functions were separated, with evaluative aspects of the latter minimized. Funds for any new demonstration or evaluation projects had been all but eliminated. Thus, the division was demoted to a unit. In a subsequent DHS reorganization with a new director, one staff member was moved out, the unit was moved into another bureau, and not even accorded the status of a separate unit. The only remnant of the evaluation function that had been so strong less than a decade before was two staff members having titles of evaluation specialists.

Analyzing Evaluation's Demise

The organizational dysfunction that occurred in DHS is certainly not unique and has been described in management literature. Many aspects fit Senge's (1990) characterization of organizational learning disabilities. The director's fixation on events, such as possible political repercussions, rather than exercise of leadership, direction, and priority-setting, was a root cause of DHS problems. Senge (1990) remarks that the irony is that despite this common fixation, most organizational threats come from slow gradual processes, not sudden events. This was certainly true at DHS. Even the crises that produced scandals could be traced to long-standing organizational neglect of mounting problems. A second disability was that without any sense of shared vision, business and finance staff focused on the specifics of their jobs (discovering possible audit exceptions and eliminating expenditures) rather than on any of the organization's larger purposes (known as the "I am my position" disability). The controls and sanctions imposed on evaluation activities reflected a "the enemy is out there" mindset. The illusion of taking charge could characterize management decisions allegedly promoting efficiency, such as freezing vacancies until a secretarial study was completed, which actually created inefficiency when indiscriminately applied to all positions.

According to Senge's laws of the fifth discipline, the learning-disabled organization is characterized by "political decision making . . . where factors other than the intrinsic merits of alternative courses of action weigh in making decisions" (p. 60). As was aptly demonstrated in DHS, he points out that the long-term consequence of such behavior is increased need for more of the same: "Ill conceived government solutions are not just ineffective, they are 'addictive' . . . fostering increased dependency and lessened abilities of local people to solve their own problems" (p. 61).

As suggested throughout the section describing attacks from within, evaluation may have been a focus because it had more diverse needs in order to carry out its functions: grants and allocations from highly specialized offices in the federal bureaucracy, contracts with universities and consultants, purchases of specialized materials such as computer hardware and software, and employment of more specialized personnel. Being perceived as a "weak sister" rather than an organization member wielding significant constituent support, regulatory power, or political influence may have also contributed to its greater vulnerability.

Additionally, the type of role and activities that characterize evaluation may have also contributed to its being perceived as part of "the enemy out there." That is, Senge (1990) notes that managers in learning-disabled organizations find collective inquiry inherently threatening. Evaluators raising difficult questions about policies and practices are rebuked in a climate of "skilled incompetence—teams full of people who are incredibly proficient at keeping themselves from learning" (p. 25). Evaluation was also a threat as an entity independent of the organization's mythical management team, receiving funding from sources outside of its control. Furthermore, preceding the attacks from within, evaluation's scope and staffing had increased considerably (in contrast to other DHS units). Limits to growth structures are often applied to expanding activities that pose threats to traditional distributions of power according to principles of balance (Senge, 1990). Finally, high levels of personal mastery and proficiency sought after in evaluation staff are rarely valued or found in a learning-disabled organization.

Implications of the Case Study. This case study describes how a politicized environment in a state human services agency affected many operations and how evaluation was particularly adversely affected, resulting in its demise and near extinction. Because politicized governmental environments are not likely to decrease at local, state, or federal levels, the case of the DHS evaluation division is worth examining for its implications.

Evaluation in human services emerged from a rational decision-making model prominent in the management literature of the 1960s: the cycle of needs assessment, planning, program development, and evaluation. The evaluation literature is still premised on a rational model: that policy makers want to solve problems, that they would rather have imperfect knowledge than none at all, that they value change and alternative ways of thinking, and that they want to know what works and what does not (Grob, 1992; Preskill, 1991; Wye and Sonnichsen, 1992). In a politicized environment, many of these traditional assumptions held by evaluators about the decision-making process may not hold true. Evaluators' assumptions about what may be appropriate for their own behaviors may similarly need profound revision. A more politicized stance may be necessary to create the constituencies who will value information or to create a mandate for policy makers to use evaluation information (Newman, Smukler, Griffin, and Fishman 1992; Wye and Sonnichsen, 1992). Compared with evaluation's youth in the 1960s, the diversity and strength of interest groups is indeed greater, including more direct consumer input in most human service fields. Developing their interest in the evaluation enterprise and their abilities to demand and use evaluation data will still be a complex and lengthy undertaking. For internal evaluators, this is risky business. Neither would statutory mandates with teeth be easy to develop. The same or different constituencies must be courted to push for these requirements. The bureaucracy and the decision-making establishment are not likely to respond enthusiastically. Such direct involvement in the political process presents a markedly different role and challenge for evaluators. The likelihood is that only evaluators outside government agencies could carry them out. Even then, they could risk sharp curtailment of any contractual work they might be asked to perform by these agencies. An even greater challenge would be limiting political involvement so that neither the credibility of the evaluator nor the objectivity (perceived or actual) of his or her work is jeopardized.

On the other hand, those with either an inherently optimistic or deterministic outlook may rely on the inevitable swing of the pendulum upwards toward a more prominent evaluation emphasis. Chelimsky (1992) informs us that "the production of accurate and timely information . . . is a truly basic function of any democratic government" (p. 29). Analysis of the development, rise, and expansion of the functions of the offices of inspector generals (IGs) at the federal level may be relevant. IGs were created by statute to perform two functions: internal and external audits of agency expenditures and criminal, civil, or administrative investigations (Moran, 1990). However, some IGs decided that they needed to add a third evaluation function, inspections. In the federal Department of Health and Human Services, such an office was created in recognition of a gap in evaluation capability. Mangano (1992) describes how this inspections function grew, began to use more rigorous research tools, and produced an incredible diversity of evaluation studies. There is controversy in the literature as to whether IG offices really do evaluations or not. If this is affirmed, IGs represent an interesting structural placement that may address the question of how evaluation mandates are framed. According to the IG Act of 1978 and its amendments (1988), the IGs operate within their departments, with access to all internal information sources, reporting to their department director. However, they are also required to have an equal reporting relationship to Congress. As such, they may operate under the best internal and external evaluation worlds.

For those who wish to take a more moderate position between political activism and a sit-and-wait approach, there may be a third option, focusing on departmental leadership. Havens (1992) argues that rebuilding federal evaluation capability rests with the executive branch, particularly with the leadership of the departments. Involvement with outside groups in identifying executive leadership candidates might thus be activist, yet less radical for evaluators. Assertions that, at the state level, a director has little ability to exercise leadership without the governor's full support (Elpers, 1989) may suggest the need for a higher level of change effort, however.

Conclusion

Evaluation has always recognized the need to take politics into account. In previous eras, however, acknowledging political realities had more to do with optimizing; for example, maximizing the likelihood of use and dissemination by having the right constituencies identified and continually involved in developing, implementing, and interpreting evaluation findings; or improving validity by incorporating value perspectives into programmatic recommendations, in addition to rationally determined costs and benefits.

However, the politics of our current realities may affect not just how well evaluation is received, but how much it is suppressed by or even eliminated from public policy actions. Evaluators and advocates for more rational and planned change activities may thus be forewarned by this case and seek to protect their enterprise through an armamentarium of their own weapons—that is, political constituencies. Wielding such armament is not without difficulties. To strike a balance of political involvement for survival with the potential for co-optation and loss of objectivity may be the challenge of the 1990s for evaluators. On the other hand, attempting to maintain a consistent presence and taking a wait-and-see attitude may not be a bad strategy while we attempt to develop and analyze new governmental structures and new evaluation identities.

References

Chelimsky, E. "Executive Branch Program Evaluation: An Upturn Soon?" In C. G. Wye and R. C. Sonnichsen (eds.), *Evaluation in the Federal Government: Changes, Trends, and Opportunities.* New Directions for Program Evaluation, no. 55. San Francisco: Jossey-Bass, 1992.

Elpers, J. R. "Development and Utilization of Incentive Systems for Mental Health Operations: Successful and Unsuccessful Knowledge Utilization in California and Los Angeles." *Journal of Mental Health Administration,* 1989, *16,* 9–20.

Garvey, G. *Facing the Bureaucracy: Living and Dying in a Public Agency.* San Francisco: Jossey-Bass, 1993.

Ginsburg, A. "Meeting the Market for Quality Evaluation in Education." In C. G. Wye and R. C. Sonnichsen (eds.), *Evaluation in the Federal Government: Changes, Trends, and Opportunities.* New Directions for Program Evaluation, no. 55. San Francisco: Jossey-Bass, 1992.

Grob, G. "How Policy Is Made and How Evaluators Can Affect It." *Evaluation Review,* 1992, *13,* 175–184.

Havens, H. S. "The Erosion of Federal Program Evaluation." In C. G. Wye and R. C. Sonnichsen (eds.), *Evaluation in the Federal Government: Changes, Trends, and Opportunities.* New Directions for Program Evaluation, no. 55. San Francisco: Jossey-Bass, 1992.

Mangano, M. F. "The Inspectors General." In C. G. Wye and R. C. Sonnichsen (eds.), *Evaluation in the Federal Government: Changes, Trends, and Opportunities.* New Directions for Program Evaluation, no. 55. San Francisco: Jossey-Bass, 1992.

Moran, W. C. "Evaluation Within the Federal Offices of Inspectors General." In M. Hendricks, M. F. Mangano, and W. C. Moran (eds.), *Inspectors General: A New Force in Evaluation.* New Directions for Program Evaluation, no. 48. San Francisco: Jossey-Bass, 1990.

Mowbray, C. T. "Getting the System to Respond to Evaluation Findings." In J. A. McLaughlin, L. J. Weber, R. W. Covert, and R. B. Ingle (eds.), *Evaluation Utilization.* New Directions for Program Evaluation, no. 39. San Francisco: Jossey-Bass, 1988.

Newman, F. L., Smukler, M., Griffin, B. P., and Fishman, D. B. "Conditions Influencing the Impact of State Level Program Evaluation: A Contrast of Two States' Evaluation of the Institute for Mental Disease Issues." *Evaluation and Program Planning,* 1992, *15,* 345–355.

Preskill, H. "The Cultural Lens: Bringing Utilization into Focus." In C. L. Larson and H. Preskill (eds.), *Organizations in Transition: Opportunities and Challenges for Evaluation.* New Directions for Program Evaluation, no. 49. San Francisco: Jossey-Bass, 1991.

Richardson, E. L. "The Value of Evaluation." In C. G. Wye and R. C. Sonnichsen (eds.), *Evaluation in the Federal Government: Changes, Trends, and Opportunities.* New Directions for Program Evaluation, no. 55. San Francisco: Jossey-Bass, 1992.

Senge, P. M. *The Fifth Discipline: The Art and Practice of the Learning Organization.* New York: Doubleday Currency, 1990.

Wye, C., and Sonnichsen, R. "Another Look at the Future of Program Evaluation in the Federal Government. Five Short Views: Chelimsky, Mangano, Wholey, Sonnichsen, and Wye." *Evaluation Practice,* 1992, *13,* 185–196.

CAROL T. MOWBRAY is associate professor and director of the research office at the Wayne State University School of Social Work.

This chapter illustrates the attempt to misuse the evaluation of a complex, large-scale, highly visible project with many powerful stakeholders and presents the authors' suggestions for countering the misuse.

Confronting Ideology and Self-Interest: Avoiding Misuse of Evaluation

Phyllis I. Vroom, Marie Colombo, Neva Nahan

Challenges and pitfalls often confront evaluators of projects designed to respond to entrenched socioeconomic problems such as structural displacement and unemployment of workers. Often, these projects have formidable sources of power undergirding them: strongly held political and social values linked to a political constituency and important coalitions who promote these values. Additionally, they may draw strength from the reputations of stakeholders. Evaluators are especially challenged when these factors are combined with the influence and credibility of a charismatic leader or project manager whose rhetoric promotes the belief that project goals are being achieved.

Deliberate or inadvertent misuse of evaluation often arises from self-interest. This self-interest is manifested in activities focused on project survival. A compelling case for survival is made by project managers: the project is the best response to the intransigent social problem; premature outcome evaluation must be avoided because it may lead to the project's demise (Rutman, 1980; Weiss and Rein, 1983). Seasoned evaluators have discussed the importance of taking account of a project's or program's ideological and political bases (Chelimsky, 1986, 1987; Rutman, 1980; Weiss, 1975) and the rationality of political responses to evaluation (Weiss, 1975).

However, awareness of the ideological context, political rationality and constraints, and players and their intents must be combined with strategies

The authors gratefully acknowledge the contributions of Sue Marx Smock, who served as technical advisor for the evaluation, and Donna Walker, who wrote and edited the evaluation report.

49

designed to continually clarify the purposes and expectations of the evaluation, to place boundaries around the project managers and staff, and to make explicit the effects of their behaviors on the evaluation of the project. We will illustrate through case example and analysis some of the strategies used by our team to mitigate against misuses of the program evaluation. Examining our mistakes, through twenty/twenty hindsight, we will identify strategies for their prevention, including the use of evaluability assessment (Muscatello, 1988; Rutman, 1980) and ongoing discussions and involvement of key stakeholders (Mowbray, 1988).

Case Illustration: Project NITCUN

We shall call the program Project NITCUN (Networking, Information, and Telecommunication for the Unemployed) to protect its identity. Project NIT-CUN was a multifaceted program organized around three primary components: a television cable communications system with employment-related programming; direct job-related and support services for the unemployed, who would gather with leaders at cable channel viewing sites; and an information and brokerage function linking the efforts of many agencies serving people with unemployment problems. Originally, the direct service component was seen by Project NITCUN as ancillary to its major function: organizing information about employment, educational, and training opportunities and agency support services (for example, health and counseling services) and rapid communication of this information to the unemployed through the cable channel. A pivotal decision early in NITCUN's development was to seek Job Training Partnership Act (JTPA) funds.

The JTPA mandate to document the placement of unemployed persons in nonsubsidized jobs added another major function to NITCUN and set the stage for conflicts about goals and priorities within NITCUN and between NIT-CUN and its funders. Throughout the life of Project NITCUN, conflict and coalitions centered around the struggle to decide whether priority should be given to the direct service component that included job placement and its documentation, or to the development of the information system devised to serve the unemployed.

Project NITCUN had six program elements: the cable channel, viewing sites for the channel, job clubs both in viewing sites and in sites not yet cabled, regional advisory groups, agency relations, and special projects. The purposes of the special projects component were to increase the audience of unemployed persons viewing the cable channel, increase attendance in the job clubs, and bring to the attention of these participants the resources of the plethora of service agencies. The agency relations component of NITCUN was responsible for developing agency resources and agreements so that information regarding employment, health, education, and social services would be made available to the unemployed through the cable channel, the job clubs, and other sources such as public libraries.

The socioeconomic and political environment that spawned and surrounded NITCUN and the ideology of its creators provides understanding both of its existence and its resultant struggles with goals, priorities, processes, and expected outcomes, and an evaluation that sought to focus these concerns.

Context and Background. During the 1970s, almost 30 percent of a midwestern state's jobs were lost to a combination of technological and market forces that radically and permanently changed its employment picture. In the early 1980s, another recession catapulted this part of the midwest into a state of crisis. The state sought innovative measures to counteract the massive economic blow, to meet the social needs of the displaced work force, and to generate new employment prospects. Calls for a bold and speedy response to the perceived crisis fostered the birth of NITCUN. The project was especially favored because of its proposal to mobilize employment-related activities in six hard-hit counties. NITCUN was begun in an atmosphere of desperation and hysteria, tempered somewhat by a belief that technological innovation was a viable approach to technologically induced crises.

The creator of NITCUN was an individual whose charisma and creativity had brought to fruition a number of complex, successful, and innovative ventures to address community needs. He mobilized his network of associates, who were leaders in strategic media (newspaper, television, and radio), business, labor, social service, employment organizations, and the regional library system. This network of associates was willing to collaborate with NITCUN's creator on a project using modern telecommunications to bring information and services to the region's unemployed. Review of early documents of NITCUN reveals, however, that the network was made up of individuals who came together out of their individual concerns about the state's unemployment; these individuals did not bring the commitment and power of their organizations to the project.

The project manager hired a team of program leaders who shared his ideological bent on organizational management and leadership. The leadership style was participatory and "antibureaucracy." With the exception of documents such as the project proposal and public relations material describing the project, lists of project staff and participating agencies, forms, and reports to document activities of the various project components did not exist or were not systematically kept. The funded proposals did document funding levels. Over its approximately two years of operation, NITCUN received nearly $2 million in JTPA funds and $200,000 from private foundations.

The Unfolding Evaluation and Project. The evaluation was commissioned by NITCUN's creator under an agreement with the chief executive officer and governing board of the sponsoring organization. The sponsoring organization viewed NITCUN as a major public service venture that might also develop and transmit knowledge about how to mobilize large-scale social interventions to address issues of public welfare. In the words of the project proposal, the broad aim of the evaluation was "not only to see what has been done and how well, but to see what could have been done and why it was or was not attempted . . . [in order to] greatly assist future policy making and management processes in the project."

Furthermore, the proposal stated that the evaluation was intended to provide feedback to NITCUN about itself, specifically by studying "1) subjective criteria such as satisfaction with services; 2) objective criteria such as participation rates, placement and performance in training and education programs, and job development, and 3) options presented during the organization and operation of [NITCUN]."

Spanning two phases of NITCUN, as specified in the funding proposal, the evaluation included examinations of system activation and system implementation over sixteen months. Two teams were involved in the evaluation. Team One focused on a process evaluation, documenting the activation of NITCUN. The team included three members: the team leader skilled in evaluation research, a second evaluator, and an anthropologist who observed and recorded routine events, behaviors, and interactions during NITCUN's startup. Team Two was hired to evaluate NITCUN's system implementation phase. This team included the three authors (one of whom was the team leader for phase one) and a technical advisor who also worked with Team One. An economist was employed by Team Two for the cost expenditure analysis.

Team One documented all aspects of the project's beginning. The anthropologist's ethnographic report was a major source of process information, describing coalitions, political issues, disagreements on goals and priorities, and power struggles among key players in the project. In retrospect, Team Two (the evaluation team) found that this report was an early indicator of the problems that were brewing from the onset of NITCUN. Both recorded and unrecorded observations of the project's unfolding explained NITCUN's failure, the misuse of the evaluation, and the foundation for some of the mistakes made by Team Two.

Evaluability Assessment of a Fluid Project. The evaluation team's first objective was to understand NITCUN and to determine whether this understanding was congruent with that of NITCUN's leadership. Thus, the team began activities to define the goals and objectives of NITCUN, to describe its program elements and organization, and to determine its desired outcomes. The product of this phase of the evaluation was to be a NITCUN program document and an evaluation design, mutually agreed on by NITCUN's leadership and the evaluation team. Data collection for this phase included interviews with the project manager, leaders of the project components (program leaders), and some members of the network of associates who formed the executive advisory committee; review of documents such as the project proposals; review of the report of Team One, including the ethnographic report; attendance at staff meetings; and attendance at meetings of the regional advisory groups in the several counties.

Additionally, the evaluation team sought to observe the job clubs and the viewing sites for the cable channel. The team also sought to obtain lists of the network of agencies involved with NITCUN. During the course of the interviews, the project manager became ill, was hospitalized, and went on medical leave for almost four months of the system implementation phase. The heads of the four major program components were defined as the project management team; no one was designated to be first among equals.

Interviews of NITCUN's leadership, including the project manager before his lengthy illness, resulted in four observations: there was disagreement about the priority of goals, there was no clear internal system of decision making, recordkeeping was unsystematized, and the leadership and project staff talked about actual program elements and projected program elements in such terms that it was difficult to discern current from planned operations. For example, when evaluation team members divided up to observe job clubs, the location and meeting times of these entities became elusive. The job clubs that were described as being active and widespread, when observed by a member of the evaluation team, were attended by fewer than five unemployed persons in two instances and only one person in another. Efforts to make appointments to observe other job clubs were not successful, although the team assiduously pursued the project manager, team members, and staff. A complete list of the agencies with which NITCUN had informal agreements was not made available. The program leader who headed agency relations proclaimed that NITCUN had informal agreements with more than 600 agencies that were either to provide resources or to serve as cable viewing sites for unemployed individuals or job clubs. Produced by NITCUN staff, after much delay, was a list of fewer than 200 agencies; only 30 of these responded to the evaluation team after repeated follow-up. Most NITCUN staff either could not or would not respond to requests from the state, the sponsoring organization, or the evaluators for documentation of spending or program activities.

A convener was brought into the project to pull together the management team and to get an actual picture of cable viewing sites that were established, job clubs in existence, and numbers of unemployed served. The ethnographic report documents that most of the staff came from activist backgrounds in grass-roots community organizations, leading to a skewing in the project's pool of skills, interests, and experience. This may account for what the evaluation team noted as the staff's and leadership's seemingly intrinsic impatience with even the most tenable bureaucratic imperatives, such as keeping records of agencies and of participation of the unemployed in job clubs and at cable viewing sites.

Lack of agreement on goals and objectives and unclear lines of authority were sources of contention among the project management team. Some team members argued that job clubs were central to the program, and that the documentation of job club participants and job placements should be required. Other team members thought that the primary goal was to get information out to displaced workers through the cable channel. The project manager continued to hold that the primary goal was the establishment of an information system and the transmission of information. Meanwhile, JTPA continued to press the sponsoring organization and the project to document the participation and job placement of displaced workers.

When the project manager returned from medical leave, the evaluation team sought to bring to the attention of NITCUN leadership the JTPA eligibility requirements for those to be served in the job clubs, as well as the reporting forms and the type of documentation required. The project manager and JTPA officials disputed the agreed-on target number of those to be served and to be employed and the forms to be used for documentation. Furthermore, JTPA withheld funds until the dispute was settled.

In a major program shift, NITCUN changed its program, deemphasizing the job clubs and emphasizing a statewide interactive cable program and conference for the unemployed, targeting displaced workers. As NITCUN changed its program and shifted its emphasis, the evaluation team modified its program document and the evaluation design. NITCUN spent the majority of its organizational time organizing and preparing for the statewide conference. The conference included bringing together unemployed people in large numbers at several viewing sites throughout the state. At these sites and at the cable station were resource people who would interact with the participants through a teleconference, informing them of employment and training opportunities and resources to meet medical, housing, financial, and other material and psychological needs, such as individual and family counseling.

Program Document and Evaluation Design. The evaluation team soon realized that, although NITCUN was funded for system implementation, it was still in the throes of system activation and suffering from lack of guidance and leadership. These observations were based on regular attendance of evaluation team members at staff meetings; information collected through interviews, project documents, and observations; and the realization, over time, of the meaning of the many missed appointments by NITCUN leadership and low attendance at cable viewing sites and job clubs.

The evaluation team faced a dilemma: to report outcomes on a project that had barely started seemed specious; not to examine outcomes would be to eschew accountability to the state and the sponsoring agency. The team hoped to tell the story of NITCUN in a balanced way. The balance would be achieved by using qualitative and quantitative approaches: quantitative measures of JTPA-defined outcomes by examining the outcomes of the job clubs and the statewide telecommunication conference; a count of the number of cable sites planned against the number achieved; a description of agency relations; and a description of cable channel viewership at home and at cable sites. Evaluation also included the description of NITCUN's organizational structure and management style and the contention between NITCUN and the state over target numbers for service and job placement. Simply measuring JTPA outcomes would not have described NITCUN and would have been unsatisfactory to the sponsoring organization and the project. For JTPA, measuring outcomes and comparing them to the outcomes of participants in other job clubs appeared sufficient. The team hoped that the evaluation would allow the major stakeholders to measure NITCUN's performance against agreed-upon standards. It hoped also to provide NITCUN with feedback on its own processes and how these processes were linked to outcomes. The evaluation team also thought that the basic question shaping NITCUN should be reexamined: that employment and problems of unemployed displaced workers could be addressed through a telecommunication information system. Certainly, the assumptions undergirding the project required review.

The evaluation team set forth a document identifying NITCUN's major goals and objectives, program components, and outcomes. There were ongoing discussions with the project manager regarding JTPA requirements interspersed with discussion of the evaluation team's view of NITCUN and the evaluation design. The project manager reiterated the centrality of the telecommunication and information systems components of NITCUN even though JTPA was the major funder. He saw the state as changing the initial agreements with him regarding the project.

Finally, the evaluation team and the project manager agreed that JTPA-related outcomes must be measured; this decision followed the revision of goals by JTPA on the number and type of unemployed to be served and, of these, the number to be placed in unsubsidized employment at a specified minimum rate of pay. The team devised reporting forms and a system of information collection so that JTPA outcomes could be measured. Additionally, measures were devised to assay the impact of the telecommunication and information system. It was not possible to use random assignment to test the efficacy of this broad-aim social intervention (Weiss and Rein, 1983). Rather, the team sought to find out the extent to which NITCUN had achieved the JTPA and state targets for service and job placement through the job clubs and the telecommunication conference and compared their results with those of job clubs that did not use the media as a major component. It also sampled unemployed workers at state unemployment offices to determine viewership of the cable channel and whether viewers used the information imparted. It described also the participation of agencies and of regional advisory groups. While data were being collected on the several program components, including data for the cost-effectiveness analysis, the evaluation team also set up appointments to interview all of the leadership and middle-management staff of NITCUN to garner their assessment of project goals and objectives, major program activities, priorities, and outcomes. In order to limit the tendency of staff to discuss the future as if it were the present, the interview schedule was structured so that staff would assess and prioritize current and, subsequently, future project components.

During this final phase of system implementation, a major dispute surfaced among the project management team and between some team members and the project manager. In dispute was the centrality of the job clubs to

NITCUN and the assertion of some staff that others were at fault for lack of coordination among program components and for other management problems. Apparently, each member of NITCUN leadership came to these "final" assessment interviews with the intention of airing his or her side of the dispute. The evaluation team found that, with one exception, program leaders were not only responsive to questions on the interview schedule but used every opportunity to offer information on the dispute without ever mentioning that a dispute was in process. The evaluation team became aware that, just as earlier, project leadership appeared to be organizing the reality of the project to shape the evaluation team's view of it. Now, each side wanted a particular point of view to be reflected in the evaluation report and so managed information through the interview. In fact, one program leader gave the evaluation team a lengthy written rebuttal to some assertions by other team members. This rebuttal highlighted this program leader's frustrations with the management style and lack of coordination from the inception of NITCUN. Earlier, program leaders, with the exception of one project team member, managed information to the evaluation team through the earlier described evasions such as missed appointments and failure to produce lists and other documents.

Afterward. As the evaluation team completed its data collection and began to write the evaluation report, NITCUN changed its program once again: it eliminated job clubs. Within months, the sponsoring organization withdrew its support and JTPA did not fund the project another year.

Strategies to Avoid Misuses and Mistakes

It took several years for the evaluation team to reflect on the NITCUN experience with any degree of equanimity. Misuse of the evaluation centered around two major activities: NITCUN's attempts to manage information about program operations through deliberate and inadvertent means, such as exaggerating numbers of participants, missing appointments, and failing to supply documents; and NITCUN's attempt to use the evaluation team as an administrative arm to design forms and collect information on project operations. Misuse of the evaluation and mistakes of the evaluation team were interrelated and centered around NITCUN's changing leadership. The evaluation team should have formally presented the evaluability assessment to NITCUN leadership; insisted on meeting periodically with project leadership collectively; determined with NITCUN who was in charge of decisions; made explicit the changes in programs and program emphases and their effect on the evaluation; and confronted earlier the evasion by program leaders of evaluator efforts to collect information.

Evaluability Assessment. Early in the evaluability assessment process, the evaluation team began to challenge some of the assumptions that undergirded the project and discerned the grandiosity of and conflict among NITCUN's goals and objectives and their lack of definition. Furthermore, the team noted the lack of clearly defined program characteristics and outcomes. For example, it was assumed that the organizations that employed the NITCUN executive advisory committee supported NITCUN when in fact committee members participated out of individual interest and not their organizations' mandate. For this reason, NITCUN's development of formal agreements with agencies took much longer than anticipated and, in some instances, agreements did not develop. It was assumed, also, that the displaced workers would have access to cable television in their homes. For some, the cost of cable was prohibitive. In one instance, there was no cable franchise in a large county with severe unemployment. The evaluation team discerned that goals and objectives were grandiose and unrealistic given the constraints of access to cable television.

It took the evaluation team longer to reach the inference that there was a pattern of evasion evident among project leadership that delayed full comprehension of the project. Development of the project document was only one component of the evaluability assessment. The most important component was negotiating the document with project leadership. The elements of the evaluability assessment have been set forth in detail elsewhere (Rutman, 1980; Muscatello, 1988). The assessment has two important components that provide opportunity for negotiations between the evaluation team and project leadership: the description of goals, objectives, characteristics, and outcomes; and decisions about the feasibility of evaluating programs or program components (Muscatello, 1988; Rutman, 1980). Not only does the program document provide opportunity for the parties to see areas of congruence and disagreement, it also sets the framework for the examination of assumptions and the evaluation design.

Periodic Meetings. Mowbray (1988) discusses the importance of meeting regularly with program managers and staff to "market the evaluation" and to influence the course of policies and the program under consideration. Establishing periodic meetings with the project management team might have been the vehicle to confront observations about management style, lack of project follow-through in submitting documents and keeping appointments, and the like. It is the vehicle for ongoing feedback. For example, NITCUN had proposed that the evaluation team provide formative information on its operations. Such information can occur only with regular and periodic feedback on project processes.

Determining the Decision-Making Structure. The adaptations in the structure of leadership due to the project manager's illness suggested early address of these changes. Rather than merely accepting the changes of the project, the evaluation team should have met with the new leadership to discuss how the management team would operate and the effects of their operation on the evaluation. The elusiveness and disagreements among members of the project management team emphasized the need to have a shared agreement on the elements of the project, or at least to determine whether shared agreement were possible. In retrospect, it seems obvious that the evaluation team was never clear about the authority structure among the project management team; it was never clear to whom one could go, ultimately, to get things done. Identifying the decision-making structure and specifying the problems in getting decisions made might have resulted in some problem solving around these issues.

Making Explicit the Impact of Goal and Program Changes. Delays in determining whether and what JTPA outcomes would be measured and changes in program and leadership resulted in delays in the development of the evaluation design and the data collection instruments. Hindsight informs the evaluation team of the need to renegotiate expectations of the evaluation or to examine whether such renegotiation is necessary when major changes occur. Expectations subject to change include evaluation report deadlines, especially when delays can be attributed to decisions within the project. The impact of delays and dramatic shifts in direction must be addressed because these events often impinge on design and the quality of the instruments developed for data collection, the timing of data collection and analysis, and the timing of the evaluation report. Negotiation of changed expectations, if any, for the evaluation and the evaluation report may be critical when deadline dates become unrealistic in light of program changes.

Confronting Evasion. Early confrontation of project staff evasion and the impact on the evaluation design would have forced project leadership to openly commit itself to evaluation or to make resistance and reservations explicit.

It took some time for the evaluation team to discern a pattern of evasion; each missed appointment, exaggerated sets of numbers, and failure to produce or extreme delays in producing documents seemed like individual acts of omission. Later, these activities appeared to be patterned, resulting in misrepresentations of project operations. Failure to address the issue was a missed opportunity to hold project staff accountable for the program and its evaluation.

Conclusion

Decisions to continue collecting process data through participant observation and interviews were important in understanding how NITCUN worked and in explaining its outcomes. The quantitative component, including the use of mailed surveys, nonequivalent comparison groups, and data collected unobtrusively through mandated forms was important documentation of what worked and what did not work given discrepancies in the description of program operations. These decisions militated against the efforts to misuse the evaluation to whitewash operations and outcomes. A conscious use of the evaluability assessment as a tool for feedback and negotiation, inclusion of the program document, clarification of the structure of decision making, early confrontation of problems with project leadership, and renegotiation of expectations in light of program changes might have been vehicles for formative feedback as well as more realistic expectations of the evaluation design. Addressing the issues that were identified in this chapter may not have ensured competent implementation of project goals and objectives or continuation of the project (Weiss, 1987). However, it might have made explicit the flaws of implementation and the faulty assumptions on which NITCUN was based. Lessons learned in the NITCUN experience have resulted in the proactive use of each of the strategies noted and recognition of the importance of evaluability assessment as a component of program evaluation.

References

Chelimsky, E. "What Have We Learned About the Politics of Program Evaluation?" *Evaluation Practice,* 1986, 8 (1), 5–21.

Chelimsky, E. "The Politics of Program Evaluation." In D. S. Cordray, H. S. Bloom, and R. J. Light (eds.), *Evaluation Practice in Review.* New Directions for Program Evaluation, no. 34. San Francisco: Jossey-Bass, 1987.

Mowbray, C. T. "Getting the System to Respond to Evaluation Findings." In J. A. McLaughlin, L. J. Weber, R. W. Covert, and R. B. Ingle (eds.), *Evaluation Utilization.* New Directions for Program Evaluation, no. 39. San Francisco: Jossey-Bass, 1988.

Muscatello, D. B. "Developing an Agenda That Works: The Right Choice at the Right Time." In J. A. McLaughlin, L. J. Weber, R. W. Covert, and R. B. Ingle (eds.), *Evaluation Utilization.* New Directions for Program Evaluation, no. 39. San Francisco: Jossey-Bass, 1988.

Rutman, L. *Planning Useful Evaluations: Evaluability Assessment.* Newbury Park, Calif.: Sage, 1980.

Weiss, C. H. "Evaluation Research in the Political Context." In E. Struening and M. Guttentag (eds.), *Handbook of Evaluation Research.* Newbury Park, Calif.: Sage, 1975.

Weiss, C. H. "Evaluating Social Programs: What Have We Learned?" *Society,* 1987, 25 (1), 40–45.

Weiss, R., and Rein, M. "The Evaluation of Broad-Aim Programs: Experimental Design, Its Difficulties, and an Alternative." In G. F. Madaus, M. Scriven, and D. L. Stufflebeam (eds.), *Evaluation Models: Viewpoints on Educational and Human Services Evaluation.* Boston: Kluwer-Nijhoff, 1983.

PHYLLIS I. VROOM is associate professor and associate dean of the School of Social Work, Wayne State University, Detroit, Michigan. She is also coordinator of the evaluation of a collaborative project between the School of Social Work and the College of Education at Wayne State University.

MARIE COLOMBO is a research coordinator of survey and evaluation services in the Center for Urban Studies, Wayne State University, Detroit, Michigan.

NEVA NAHAN is program director of survey and evaluation services at the Center for Urban Studies at Wayne State University.

Misuse of an evaluation occurs when the process or findings are altered to promote one's self-interests; this generally occurs when educational programs have difficulty demonstrating their impact on the target population.

The Misuse of Evaluation in Educational Programs

Micah Dial

This chapter discusses evaluation misuse in educational programs. Presented here are three scenarios in which misuse occurred and an attempt to identify how it occurred, by whom, for what purpose, and how it might have been avoided. All three scenarios were actual cases in which the author served as the program evaluator. In closing, some thoughts are given regarding the misuse of program evaluation, specifically related to education.

In any misuse of evaluation, those responsible can be identified. They can include the evaluator, another evaluator, the evaluator's supervisor, the program directors, the program clients, the funding source, the legislators, the media, or the directors of competing programs. In essence, anyone who has a stake in the evaluation and the evaluation results has reason to wrongfully influence the outcomes of an evaluation. Also identifiable is the way in which an evaluation is misused. Readers are probably able to compose a comprehensive list. A partial list includes intentionally changing the written report, tabling the report, stopping the evaluation before it is completed, changing evaluators, assigning an inept evaluator, withholding information, "cooking" the data, or even requesting the evaluation at a particular time.

After considering evaluations that I personally conducted, both as an internal and external evaluator, where the evaluation itself or its results were misused, I have come to one primary conclusion regarding evaluation misuse: misuse of an evaluation occurs when the process or the findings are altered to promote one's self-interests. This occurs largely because of the difficulty in showing a positive impact of programs on their targeted populations.

Finally, there are some suggestions to combat the misuse of evaluations. Although many aspects of decision-making and policy-making processes are beyond the control of evaluators, the awareness of evaluation misuse is valuable.

Scenario One: A Program Director's Manipulation

This first scenario concerns a program designed for the in-house training and certifying of teachers. It was the first project assigned to a newly hired evaluator within an internal evaluation department at a large school district. At the first meeting, the program director could not say into how many classrooms or schools the program's interns were placed and, thereby, how many students they affected. She could not say how many teachers had been certified through the program in its first seven years of existence, nor even how many interns were in the program at the present time. She could not even say how many people were employed in the department. Before long, it seemed that the program director certainly must know these things about the program, but she had no intention of cooperating with the evaluation. At every request for data or clarification, the program personnel were not cooperative or were manipulative.

Records were not made available. In fact, the department was not computerized. One of the recommendations for the program was that the department be computerized. Interns complained that they had to resubmit their documents (such as letters of reference and university transcripts) because they had been lost in the department. Another recommendation was that the training needed to be reviewed. Many interns found the training aspects boring and a waste of their time.

There were few other recommendations. Overall, the report presented positive conclusions about the program. On every variable on which some data could be collected, the program's interns were as good as, or above, their non-program peers. These variables included certification scores, classroom appraisal scores, students' academic achievement, and teacher retention. With the rather positive report, it seemed odd that the program director complained about the few recommendations. She tried vehemently to manipulate the report and even have the recommendations removed. The assistant director also told the evaluator to be careful of the director's influence, stating that she was quite powerful within the district.

Perhaps the main problem with programs such as this is that there is little or no accountability nor is there an incentive to cooperate with evaluations. The majority of programs are rubber-stamped, receiving annual approval and continued funds from the district, state, or federal level. The evaluation department rarely reported negative findings on programs. This may be because of the political nature of an internal evaluation department of a governmental entity. The supervisors in the evaluation department, after consulting with the program director, were not going to release the report. Fortunately, both supervisors were on vacation at the time of its final review and the division head would not allow the director's complaints to delete the recommendations from the report.

This program is not inherently bad. The idea of the program is potentially a good one. There are a number of reasons for the actions of the program personnel that will not be discussed in detail here (such as the pressure to recruit minority teachers, regardless of qualifications, and the pressure from the district administration to increase the number of district-trained interns). Such things are perhaps the reasons for what eventually happened to this program. After an exposé by an investigative reporter from a local television station, the program was halted, the director, assistant director, and four clerks were fired, and investigations are being conducted by the state education agency, the immigration service, the local district attorney, and the school district. The charges were corruption and mismanagement, stating that things were done (such as job placements, alteration of files, and coaching on testing) in return for bribes by the intern candidates.

This was a blatant example of misuse on the behalf of the program personnel. In hindsight, the reasons were the self-preservation and personal gains of the staff. In this case, the organization was too political to evaluate itself. This evaluation project might have best been served by an external evaluator or by stronger support from the organization for the evaluation, allowing for complete access and disclosure of information.

Scenario Two: An Administrator's Political Agenda

This scenario involved the evaluation of the districtwide implementation of a state-mandated program. The goal of the program was to provide tutorial services to students. Passed as part of a state education bill, it mandated that each school must make tutoring available to low-achieving students. No funds were provided by the state to the districts, and transportation did not have to be provided by the districts. In the law as it was codified, every student who was scoring 70 or below on a scale of 100 in one of the main subject areas (mathematics, science, social studies, and language arts) was eligible for the program. However, there were two reasons that, in practice, made the program available for all students: because funds were not provided by the state, there could be no complaints that money was inappropriately spent on noneligible students; and as in similar programs, if such services were being provided to some students, the district made them available to all.

When the tutorial program began in the district where the internal evaluation was to be conducted, the superintendent was enthusiastic. A name was given to the district's version of the program, more than a million dollars was made available for program implementation, and a director was appointed. During the first year, the program was implemented in only five senior high schools. The next year, it was decided that all 240 schools within the district would implement the program. Some schools provided tutors (usually teachers who were paid overtime) before the school day, after the regular school day, or on Saturday mornings. Also, there was a district requirement that at least fifteen students enroll before a class could be made available.

The program's difficulties began one Saturday morning. Not understanding that students were not required to attend, the superintendent ordered truant officers and state troopers to collect the students. After an outcry from parents in one particular low-income ethnic minority school, there was news coverage by the local media, including segments on the evening television news. People in this particular community claimed that the superintendent's actions were motivated by prejudice. After this, the superintendent ignored the program, failed to support any aspect of it, and made derogatory remarks about the program.

When the evaluation was requested, a supervisor stated to the newly employed internal evaluator that the superintendent did not like the program and that it was common knowledge that the program did not work. The evaluator was told not to hold back and to report negative findings. As site visits began, the program director stated that the superintendent and the evaluation department, specifically the supervisor and the department head, were out to destroy the program. The analysis of students' end-of-year academic achievement data indicated no positive impact on the test scores and course grades of the program participants. In fact, the grades of those in the program dropped at a much higher rate than those of a matched sample of nonparticipants.

Funds were cut every year for the five years that the program existed. The superintendent's last budget, before she left for another job, completely cut the budget for the program and dissolved the program director's position. In hindsight, despite similar results of other programs, this was the only negative report that came from the internal evaluation department over a number of years.

This evaluation was misused from the initial request to the final report. Although much of this misuse was beyond the control of the evaluator, background of the program and awareness of the political nature of the program would have been valuable. Also, the district might have been better served by an external evaluator in this case, preferably one who reported directly to the school board. This might have circumvented the politics involved at the evaluation department's or superintendent's level.

Scenario Three: An Evaluator and Personal Influences

This scenario involved the evaluation of the statewide implementation of a federally funded program. The goal of the program was to help initiate technical education in secondary and postsecondary schools. In the course of the evaluation, colleges and schools within each area of the state were visited. In a few schools, the administrator (usually a college dean or school principal) informed the evaluator that the state or federal bureaucrats were of no concern to them, and that they wanted nothing to do with them (the bureaucrats).

When such is the attitude of a program director, how does this affect the evaluation? The first consideration is the effect on the program itself. In some programs, there may or may not have been compliance with the law that allocated funds. However, there was a measurable positive impact on the program participants, even if the impact was not the program's intended one. In other programs, the director's negative attitude toward the state or federal agency was evident in the lack of compliance with the mandates. However, in this second group of programs, there was little or no evidence that anything was being provided for the targeted population.

The question for this scenario is, Does an evaluator misuse his or her role if the evaluation of these two types of programs are treated differently? Neither are necessarily complying with the mandated structure and other rules of the program. At one site, however, the evaluator maintains a positive view of the program and its director, whose comments are, "They (bureaucrats) do not know what is needed in our area," and "I will do what is best for our students and our community." If the schools maintain a high level of academic achievement, it is difficult not to admire such achievement. On the other hand, despite a similar attitude shown by the program director, another program clearly provides no evidence of anything that is being done for the targeted population. These results give the evaluator a negative attitude toward this program.

After considering this situation, it is concluded that the fact that an evaluator identifies with or admires the achievements of a service provider is not necessarily an abuse of the evaluator's role. However, when one program is rewarded or recognized over another because of the personal or political similarities of the director and the evaluator, then the evaluator has indeed misused his or her role.

This scenario certainly does not indicate an obvious abuse of position. Yet experience has been that, more often than not, manipulations are subtle and the slanting of evaluation results are also subtle. Indeed, it is the culmination of many such seemingly innocent and insignificant personal value judgments throughout evaluation projects that leads to the final conclusions. Although evaluators often see a program director's manipulation (many times during the first meeting), evaluators are perhaps less likely to observe the influences of their own biases. Thus, to combat this type of misuse, evaluators should make a conscious effort to periodically question themselves regarding how their personal preferences may be influencing the evaluation results.

Reasons for Evaluation Misuse in Educational Programs

The majority of educational programs do not work. It has been stated so often that it may be considered an axiom regarding educational and other social programs. To state it perhaps more appropriately, in the majority of educational programs, it is very difficult to show a measurable increase in the desired program outcomes. Such a conclusion is based not only on references of others, but on personal experience. There are many reasons for the lack of effectiveness of these programs. Often, their targeted populations are of low socioeconomic status from neighborhoods with few positive role models. Often, resources to fund the programs are inadequate. Just as often, educational programs are actually combating noneducational social problems. Many people

do not realize that, in some regions, schools are given the responsibility to provide food, clothing, health care, shelter, and counseling in addition to education. When cast in this light, it may be more surprising that any programs ever
show a positive educational impact on the lives of the participants.

Perhaps a blatant statement regarding the ineffectiveness of programs is
too harsh. After all, schools are open. The majority of children do learn to read
and write. The majority of students do attend on a regular basis and eventually graduate with basic skills. It is assumed that the same could be said for
other areas such as law and health care. Courts and hospitals are open. Trials
are conducted and surgeries are performed. Not only are services rendered,
but a positive impact for the clients and patients is often seen. If this is the case,
how can we say that the programs do not work? The reason may lie in the distinction between a temporary program and a permanent institution. In education, there are local, state, and federal programs, many of which are intended
to serve as initiatives to begin what is considered a positive effort for the program participants, to be continued by local funds or incorporated into the local
system. Perhaps the difficulty in these programs is simply the difficulty of cre-
ating change. Whatever the reasons for the failure of educational programs to
show a positive impact, program ineffectiveness may lead to one of the primary
reasons for misuse of evaluations. That is, self-interests (namely, self-preservation and self-promotion) of the stakeholders become exaggerated when there
is little evidence of program effectiveness. There are many reasons why clients
may or may not accept the results of evaluation research (Carter, 1973). Self-
interest is at the heart of the matter.

Education Week (Rothman, 1993) ran a lead story in which the work of
educational research centers and regional laboratories was "marred by design
and methodological problems" (p. 1). Methodology, like evaluation use, has
been one of the primary topics of the literature. Often, complaints about evaluations (often disagreements with evaluation findings) report that there were
methodological flaws. This chapter has discussed a more esoteric side of evaluation: the human aspect. The misuses of educational program evaluation are
generally not due to methodological issues. Rather, intentions of the stakeholders is the issue. In the three cases discussed here, the primary cause of misuse was the self-interest of a stakeholder.

In large part, what one receives by acquiring an evaluator is some objectivity. Objectivity means merely that someone outside the program's purview is
brought in to provide an outsider's perspective. Although, as has been stated,
evaluators (and all researchers) bring their own biases to each project, one hopes
that, at the very least, the evaluator is not a primary stakeholder in the program
itself. It is when this objectivity is influenced by self-interest that an evaluator
misuses his or her role. When any stakeholder attempts to influence an evaluation or alter the findings to promote his or her self-interests, it is a misuse of
evaluation. "Even the best evaluation may go unused if a decision-maker senses
that such use will undermine his personal situation" (King, 1988, p. 289).

What Can Be Done? What can be done to combat the misuse of evaluation processes and evaluation findings? Considering the examples provided here, a few recommendations are offered. First, external evaluations may be more reliable than internal evaluations in cases where internal politics interfere with the evaluation. "Clout within an organization exerts a powerful influence on the conduct of evaluation and the use of evaluation results" (King, 1988, p. 289). In the scenarios presented here, the ability of external evaluators to remain outside of the internal politics may have helped to prevent misuse.

Second, whether external or internal, evaluations should report directly to the funding source. An external evaluator should report to the foundation instead of the program directors. In the case of school districts, internal evaluators should report directly to the school board. Although these structures have their own inherent difficulties, they are preferable to the alternatives. Conner (1988) noted that organizational location is important and suggested that direct links to decision makers be established and maintained.

Finally, evaluators should periodically question themselves throughout an evaluation to determine whether their own biases are wrongly influencing the evaluation process or findings. Regarding the deliberate misuse of evaluation, Raizen and Rossi (1981) wrote, "The best that evaluators . . . can do is to make sure through review of evaluations that those that are defective are clearly identified and that exemplary evaluations are also clearly identified. Full publicity should be given to the evaluation review procedure and its results" (p. 102). An evaluator's awareness of misuse and the factors involved (that is, who is misusing the evaluation and for what purpose) is perhaps the best recommendation.

References

Carter, R. K. "Clients' Resistance to Negative Findings." *School Evaluation: The Politics & Process.* Berkeley, Calif.: McCutchan Publishing Corporation, 1973.

Conner, R. F. "Structuring Knowledge Production Activities to Facilitate Knowledge Utilization: Thoughts on Important Utilization Issues." *Studies in Educational Evaluation,* 1988, *14,* 273–283.

King, J. A. "Research on Evaluation Use and Its Implications for Evaluation Research and Practice." *Studies in Educational Evaluation,* 1988, *14,* 285–299.

Raizen, S. A., and Rossi, P. H. (eds.). *Program Evaluation in Education: When? How? To What Ends?* Washington, D.C.: National Academy Press, 1981.

Rothman, R. "Study Cites Need to Improve E.D. Research Efforts." *Education Week,* 1993, *12* (32), 1–24.

MICAH DIAL is senior research consultant for Evaluation & Data Analysis Services, Inc., Houston, Texas.

Limited understanding of the purposes of program evaluation can lead to misuse; evaluators must educate clients and stakeholders so that evaluation designs are refined to produce useful information.

Misusing Program Evaluation by Asking the Wrong Question

Emil J. Posavac

Resistance to evaluation on the part of program staff, administrators, and program participants is a repeated theme in the evaluation literature (Posavac and Carey, 1992). Many reasons are given for such resistance; however, it can be argued that the core reason for resistance is fear of evaluation. Often evaluators dismiss this fear without carefully assessing why people fear evaluation. Is fear of evaluation to be expected? All people evaluate the effectiveness of their activities—cooks taste food while preparing it, carpenters run their hands over the wood they have been sanding before staining it, we calculate the balance of our checking accounts before writing checks, hospital physicians monitor the progress of their patients through laboratory tests, and so on. Because self-evaluation is so common, it must be useful. Why, then, would people resist program evaluation?

Program evaluation has often been imposed on programs. However, the requirement to evaluate a program is not, in itself, the source of the fear and resistance. The source is the requirement combined with a limited view of the purpose of program evaluation that leads to this tragic situation. This chapter illustrates the common assumption that program evaluations are carried out solely to place a good/bad stamp on programs; I argue that it is this assumption that creates fear, which often leads to resistance, which, in turn, can render the program evaluation ineffective. This problem is especially lethal when the evaluator, despite good intentions, fails to recognize the limited view of program evaluation held by program-level stakeholders. The chapter ends with several suggestions evaluators may use as antidotes to these toxic assumptions.

NEW DIRECTIONS FOR PROGRAM EVALUATION, no. 64, Winter 1994 © Jossey-Bass Publishers

Why the Thought of Evaluation Evokes Fear

The most common experience people have with evaluation is getting grades in school. For many people, memories of getting grades and scores from standardized tests are quite unpleasant. It is not surprising that they dislike the idea of evaluation. Although the idea of program evaluation is becoming more well-known, it is often confused with being graded.

Second, it is common to avoid criticism whenever we can. Program managers and staff are just as sensitive to criticism as others and they do not lose this sensitivity when they enter their program sites. The fact is that we benefit greatly when we receive criticism or even anticipate it. The likelihood of my discovering gaps in the logic of material I have written increases when I simply imagine someone else reading what I have written. Scriven (1981) comments: "If you value quality, reach out for suggestions to those who think you *lack* it" (p. 50). It is one thing, of course, to agree with Scriven in the abstract and quite another thing to act on his suggestion.

People also fear evaluation when they believe that they are losing control of important aspects of their lives. Work life is essential for earning a living and often an important aspect in self-definition. A sense of control is crucial in good adjustment (Taylor, 1991). Some aspects of retaining a sense of control in work life include being able to predict accurately what is expected and the freedom to follow well-practiced procedures or to innovate when new procedures promise better results. Managers prize predictability very highly (Dobyns and Crawford-Mason, 1991). Contrast this orientation with the credo of evaluators. Evaluators come into a setting consciously holding the values of flexibility and openness to new ideas, without allegiance to past practices and assumptions common to the program setting. Evaluators are quite willing to entertain the idea that the program is not achieving what the program staff thinks it is. If an external evaluation is mandated, program-level people may suspect that the evaluators have considerable power with those who control the funds for the program. When stakeholders believe that evaluators do not respect their expertise and may have a hand in the program's destiny, they are going to fear the evaluation and attempt to regain control by determining the outcome of the evaluation. When such a negative situation develops, it is not surprising to learn that program-level stakeholders believe that the sole purpose of a program evaluation is to draw a good/bad conclusion about the program.

Is This View of Evaluation Irrational?

Although this common negative view of evaluation may be unproductive, there are reasons for its development. Many people remember classroom evaluations that were made without clear criteria of success. Many students still receive grades on papers without any explanations of the reasons for the assigned grades and without any guidance for improvement. Without specified criteria or guidance for future efforts, grading may seem arbitrary and, consequently, may evoke fear.

In the public sector, there is a sense that evaluation is designed to get the "bad guys." A former governor of Illinois was quoted as saying, "Very rarely does one see anything in the media about program evaluation unless it has to do with a scandal" (Palumbo, 1987, p. 23). Many forms of systematic evaluation of medical care have had similar punitive assumptions. Kritchevsky and Simmons (1991) commented, "Currently, most medical quality programs are designed to prevent future bad occurrences by punishing past ones. The goal of much medico-legal action is openly punitive. The natural tendency, given this environment, is to hide or avoid responsibility for bad outcomes. If punished for them, people will choose to hide mistakes rather than openly discuss them as a springboard for system development" (p. 1822).

These examples can be multiplied, but the point has been made that for many people, personal experience with evaluation has been negative because evaluation has been limited to labeling performances or products as good or bad rather than focusing on approaches to improvement. The effects of these experiences are evident when program-level stakeholders are asked to participate in determining the design of a program evaluation. Because their experiences and views of evaluation are so limited, they often suggest evaluation designs that would lead to bottom-line conclusions when they really need help in refining their programs.

Summative or Formative Evaluation?

There are two general purposes of program evaluation: summative and formative. Both have their place and both are essential. Most people have experiences with summative evaluation; getting grades for a course is an example. The purpose is to label the student's achievement as good, adequate, or inadequate. On the other hand, evaluation can have a different purpose: the improvement of the activity. Students could receive information on how they can improve their work regardless of the level of skill they have already achieved. This would be called a formative evaluation. These two purposes of student evaluation are different even though they use the same outcome variable, student skill level. (For a fuller description of the purposes of program evaluation, see Posavac and Carey, 1992.)

Both kinds of program evaluation are needed, but many stakeholders seem to ignore the conditions making one or the other appropriate. Imagine you are looking for a nice meal. What kind of evaluation would most interest you? The crucial determinant of the type of evaluation needed is whether you intend to buy the meal in a restaurant or to prepare it yourself. If you are looking for a good restaurant, you would want summative evaluations. Friends whose tastes and values you trust or food experts could be asked for recommendations of restaurants they liked and warnings about restaurants they did not like. You would have absolutely no concern about how the disliked restaurants could improve their services or recipes. On the other hand, if you are preparing a meal yourself, you would engage in a great deal of formative evaluation. You would want to monitor the temperature and the length of time for cooking; you would often taste the foods being prepared in order to make corrections in the seasonings. You would seek information in order to guide and correct your efforts. Because you are responsible for the meal, you would not reject any useful information. You would want to know if something is going wrong; if you see smoke from a pan, you would check to see whether something is burning. Although you are hoping for a favorable summative evaluation in the end, your primary concern is to be sure you obtain enough information to guide you toward your goal of having a nice meal.

The major concern of this chapter is problems created by forgetting the need for formative evaluation when evaluators are working with stakeholders who have a part in designing and implementing the program. Before focusing on helping stakeholders understand how formative evaluation can help them, a few comments on the conditions that require summative evaluations will keep later comments in context.

Consumer Choices. A well-known magazine, *Consumer Reports,* provides an excellent illustration of summative evaluation. The magazine describes the characteristics of various brands of an item, such as cars or stereo speakers, and then rates them on a variety of dimensions of quality. Although one or another characteristic may make a particular brand attractive to a buyer with specific needs, the magazine usually combines quality on the various dimensions to rank the brands from best to worst. At times, the magazine will label a good model with an attractive price as a "Best Buy" and sometimes a model with particular problems is labeled "Unacceptable." In a similar fashion, whenever one must choose among several completed products or programs, one can make use of summative evaluations. A legislative body or an organization CEO may need to make a choice between funding program A or program B. A school district makes decisions about adopting one or another textbook.

These situations share a common feature: the potential consumer has no hand in developing the product and has only a very indirect part to play in any possible future changes in the product. When these conditions are met, a summative evaluation is needed.

Summative evaluations may also be needed when there is evidence of villainy or incompetence. Such situations are similar to making consumer choices in that there is reason to believe that the individuals carrying out the program would not or could not make use of information to make program improvements.

Evidence that Stakeholders Confuse the Two Purposes of Evaluation. My experiences as an evaluator are largely confined to educational and medical care settings. In both settings, stakeholders who wanted to learn more about their programs or programs that they believed in made requests for evaluations in words that sounded as though they wanted summative evaluations.

As a consultant, I worked with a director of a rehabilitation unit in a hospital; I'll call him Dr. Smith. Dr. Smith approached the research and evaluation unit of the hospital for an evaluation. He phrased his charge to the evaluators in approximately these words: we want to know whether we really help these patients; are we making a difference? This sounded like a request for a summative evaluation. This was some years ago; at that time I did not understand yet that stakeholders sometimes seem to request types of evaluations that they really do not want or need. The evaluation team set out to find a good comparison group in a neighboring hospital. After making an arrangement to gather data in a hospital without a rehabilitation unit, Dr. Smith objected to the plan. He began to argue that the benefits of rehabilitation are well-known and fully documented. The initial high level of cooperativeness disappeared; fear and resistance became evident. A search of Medline revealed that if there were documented comparison or controlled studies of the effectiveness of rehabilitation units similar to Dr. Smith's, the studies were very old or in very obscure journals. Knowledge of the dearth of evaluations of similar rehabilitation units did not alter his view that what the evaluators thought he wanted was not needed. Although he had used summative language, he had never wanted a summative evaluation.

A more recent example comes from a university setting. A series of workshops was designed to help natural scientists from a variety of colleges and universities learn how to teach principles of ethics in their classes. The potential funding agency insisted that an evaluation plan accompany the proposal. The initial design for the evaluation was a purely summative evaluation. Instead of proposing to observe the workshops, to interview participants and leaders, to examine course syllabi of participants, or to learn how participants shared their experiences with their colleagues on their home campuses, the initial design focused solely on whether the students of participants knew more about ethics than students of nonparticipants. Although that is one ultimate goal of the workshops, such comparisons would, at best, permit one to conclude that the workshop series was good or bad and nothing more. It would provide no information about what went well and what went poorly, no suggestions for improving the workshops, and no documentation that the workshops were even held. Although that last concern may seem facetious, there is evidence that programs have been "evaluated" that were never implemented (Patton, 1980; Rossi, 1978). Furthermore, it is common knowledge among experienced evaluators that programs are seldom implemented as designed (Majchrzak, 1986). Similarly, physicians treating outpatients must remember that many ill people do not comply with the treatments that have been prescribed (Posavac and others, 1985).

The ethics workshop developers agreed to a summative evaluation plan that could not help them to learn anything about the quality of their efforts.

The criterion of success, the knowledge of students of the workshop participants, is so far removed from the activities of the program that no one could
have ever found even a hint of what had worked poorly had the evaluation
been unfavorable or what had succeeded had the evaluation been favorable.
The limitations of such a summative evaluation unfortunately often become
apparent to stakeholders only after a report has been written and people ask
"So what?" after reading it. Carrying through with such an evaluation would
be a clear misuse of evaluation resources.

A Better Approach

A better model to follow in most settings is the practice of physicians following the effects of a hospital-based treatment plan. There is a clear parallel
between formative program evaluation and medical testing. (This parallel was
initially suggested to me by Raymond G. Carey, vice president for quality measurement, Lutheran General Hospital, Park Ridge, Ill.) After making a diagno-
sis and beginning treatment, physicians examine the reactions of the patient
using additional medical tests. A physician expects the treatment to have certain physical effects on the patients that help them to return to better health
and fuller social functioning (Kaplan, 1990). Although the ultimate measure
of the effectiveness of hospital care is the degree to which patients can return
to carrying out their roles in their homes, at work, and in the community,
physicians would be seriously remiss if they ignored all the intermediate steps
that must be completed successfully before their patients are to achieve their
ultimate goals.

Staying with this analogy for a moment, consider what physicians should
conclude if the blood and other tests reveal that the expected improvements
are not occurring. If the treatment is being implemented, but signs of improvement do not appear, something must change. Physicians must consider
whether the patient had been misdiagnosed or whether the treatment is not
sufficiently aggressive or whether this particular patient will not respond to the
treatment regimen chosen. In other words, if the intermediate steps in the
patient's recovery do not occur, the condition being treated and the treatment
must be reconsidered. Under no circumstances would the physician denigrate
the laboratory technicians for returning unwelcome news.

Now suppose that the blood and other tests indicate improvement but the
patient does not return to better function. This implies that the patient has an
additional problem that was not observed at first. Although the treatment may
have been appropriate, the problem is more complex than initially believed.
The problem may be physical or even psychological; additional diagnostic
work must be done.

It is not unknown for a physician to blame a patient for failing to return
to function after the physician provided the treatment thought to be appropriate. Although at times it may be a patient's psychological state that now

needs improvement, at other times the physician may be seeking an excuse for his or her inability to develop an effective treatment. This exception to the productive use of information for formative purposes in medical settings shows that even quite objective information may be rejected when it threatens a provider's sense of control.

Recognizing the essential contribution medical tests make in evaluating medical treatment does not require great leaps of imagination. Readers will recognize parallels to social programs. For example, job training programs that fail to impart job skills that are needed by employers cannot be expected to help participants to gain employment. The problem may lie in the choice of curriculum, the method of teaching, the thoroughness of the classes, or the motivation of the trainees. Other programs are designed to develop knowledge of how diseases are spread in order to lead people to avoid high-risk behaviors; however, even when knowledge increases, the programs have not led to changes in levels of high-risk behavior (Weisse, Nesselhof-Kendall, Fleck-Kandath, and Baum, 1990). Clearly, the intervention was insufficient because the causes of high-risk behavior were not understood. In the first example, the work skills must be taught better or the curriculum must be adjusted; in the second example, the theory connecting knowledge to high-risk behavior is inadequate. In both cases, assistance is needed to improve the program; providing only summative information would be a misuse of evaluation services.

What Can Evaluators Do About Misunderstandings of the Purposes of Program Evaluation?

Recognizing that a client may seem to want summative evaluation but really needs formative evaluation is a good place to begin. Evaluators can take an active role in helping their clients to understand what they really need.

Educate Clients. Evaluators can define the purposes of summative and formative evaluation for clients. Many stakeholders hold a summative model implicitly, but recognize the benefits of getting information that could point to program improvement once they realize that evaluation can make such contributions. This suggestion does not mean that an evaluation can only be summative or formative. In fact, the best evaluations include both purposes.

Ask Clients How They Might Use an Evaluation. Some clients may suggest a summative evaluation and indicate that a negative evaluation will mean that they must replan the entire program. If that is so, then an evaluation that included data suggesting directions for program improvement would give them a head start if they need to redesign their program. For example, if an inadequate analysis of needs had been carried out before program implementation, an evaluation that included a better examination of participant needs might be useful. It might be suggested that a reexamination of needs would be helpful because the program is in place and the specific people seeking services can be reached directly. If, on the other hand, the goal is to obtain data supporting the effectiveness of the service that will become part of a request for financial support or program expansion, it may well be that a summative evaluation is precisely what is needed.

Suggest Possible Findings of an Evaluation. Evaluators should not be surprised that people contract for an evaluation without ever imagining that the evaluation will be anything but positive. Before agreeing on an evaluation design, it might be useful to ask what program managers and staff would do on the basis of various results of evaluations. One might ask the stakeholders to imagine a favorable outcome. Then one would ask what use the stakeholders will make of the findings. Can the findings be used to improve services or streamline procedures? My guess is that favorable summative evaluations will not yield suggestions about directions to improve the organization. When that is true, the evaluator can raise the possibility of gathering additional information to help understand why the service works so that the stakeholders can retain what is crucial to making it effective while working on refinements.

An important goal of suggesting possible negative outcomes would be to learn whether an unfavorable summative evaluation would be greeted with confusion and refusal to accept the findings. When this occurs, clearly the evaluation should be redesigned to provide data that will prove credible. On the positive side, if the only good result is to redesign the program, the evaluator might suggest gathering additional data that could help to jump-start that process.

This strategy of discussing the use of possible outcomes can help the stakeholder to think of additional variables that should be observed and to elaborate and refine additional theories relating program activities to desired outcomes. (See Bickman, 1987 and 1990, and Lipsey, 1993, on the advantages of working on the theoretical underpinnings of programs.) The objective in asking these hypothetical questions is to help the evaluator and stakeholders match the evaluation design to actual needs of the program manager and staff, thus avoiding the misuse of resources.

In raising the specter of a negative summative evaluation, evaluators must proceed with great tact. Recall the earlier comments about the contrast between the skeptical stance of evaluators and the commitment of service providers. The openness of the evaluator to unfavorable evaluations can be threatening to program-based stakeholders, but their participation in designing an effective evaluation will be enhanced when they can imagine negative evaluation findings.

Reassure the Program-Based Stakeholders. Working through learning what is potentially of most use to program-based stakeholders could have the effect of reassuring them that they are in control of their program. If the evaluation is for program improvement, they need to know that they are in control. They also need to know that when the evaluation is appropriately structured to meet their information needs, the probability of their remaining in control of the program is increased. In contrast, providing an unwanted summative evaluation may have the side effect of reducing their control of the program.

Summary

The misuse of evaluation by asking the wrong questions has been called a third type of design error by Dunn (1982). Dunn argued that many presentations of program evaluation procedures have been limited to developing valid research designs and statistical analyses with sufficient power to detect program effects. Such presentations remain necessary but, as Dunn pointed out, additional concern needs to be placed in meeting the needs of program staff and funding organizations. The present chapter particularly fits Dunn's category of "threats to relevance"; however, I argue that program stakeholders themselves can be the source of threats to relevance when they hold a very limited view of program evaluation. The concern about the gathering of information that will permit staff members to improve services is also found in developments to apply statistical process control in service settings (Berwick, Godfrey, and Roessner, 1990). Statistical process control procedures help workers to get the process right and to maintain it rather than waiting to inspect the final product to see whether it is good or bad.

The most effective evaluators take an active role in educating stakeholders about program evaluation in an effort to reduce the inappropriate fear of program evaluation and to increase its usefulness. This chapter has focused on the common perception that evaluation must be summative when, in fact, formative evaluations are usually of more use to program managers and staff. One central service evaluators can provide is to show stakeholders when summative evaluations are needed and when formative evaluations are needed. Helping clients to understand this distinction and helping them to develop evaluations with an appropriate balance between formative and summative purposes is a major contribution evaluators can make toward reducing the misuse of evaluation.

References

Berwick, D. M., Godfrey, A. B., and Roessner, J. *Curing Health Care: New Strategies for Quality Improvement*. San Francisco: Jossey-Bass, 1990.

Bickman, L. (ed.). *Using Program Theory in Evaluation*. New Directions for Program Evaluation, no. 33. San Francisco: Jossey-Bass, 1987.

Bickman, L. (ed.). *Advances in Program Theory*. New Directions for Program Evaluation, no. 47. San Francisco: Jossey-Bass, 1990.

Dobyns, L., and Crawford-Mason, C. *Quality or Else: The Revolution in World Business*. Boston: Houghton Mifflin, 1991.

Dunn, W. N. "Reforms as Arguments." *Knowledge: Creation, Diffusion, Utilization*, 1982, 3 (3), 293–326.

Kaplan, R. M. "Behavior as the Central Outcome in Health Care." *American Psychologist*, 1990, 45 (11), 1211–1220.

Kritchevsky, S. B., and Simmons, B. P. "Continuous Quality Improvement: Concepts and Practices for Physician Care." *JAMA*, 1991, 266 (13), 1817–1823.

Lipsey, M. W. "Theory as Method: Small Theories of Treatments." In L. B. Sechrest and A. G. Scott (eds.), *Understanding Causes and Generalizing about Them*. New Directions for Program Evaluation, no. 57. San Francisco: Jossey-Bass, 1993.

Majchrzak, A. "Keeping the Marines in the Field." *Evaluation and Program Planning,* 1986, 9 (3), 253–265.

Palumbo, D. J. (ed.). *The Politics of Program Evaluation.* Newbury Park, Calif.: Sage, 1987.

Patton, M. Q. *Qualitative Evaluation Methods.* Newbury Park, Calif.: Sage, 1980.

Posavac, E. J., and Carey, R. G. *Program Evaluation: Methods and Case Studies,* 4th ed. Englewood Cliffs, N.J.: Prentice Hall, 1992.

Posavac, E. J., Sinacore, J. M., Brotherton, S. E., Helford, M., and Turpin, R. S. "Increasing Compliance to Medical Treatment Regimens." *Evaluation and the Health Professions,* 1985, 8 (1), 7–22.

Rossi, P. H. "Issues in the Evaluation of Human Services." *Evaluation Quarterly,* 1978, 2 (4), 573–599.

Scriven, M. *Evaluation Thesaurus.* (3rd ed.) Inverness, Calif.: Edgepress, 1981.

Taylor, S. E. *Health Psychology,* rev. ed. New York: McGraw-Hill, 1991.

Weisse, C. S., Nesselhof-Kendall, S.E.A., Fleck-Kandath, C., and Baum, A. "Psychosocial Aspects of AIDS Prevention Among Heterosexuals." In J. Edwards, R. S. Tindale, L. Heath, and E. J. Posavac (eds.), *Social Influence Processes and Prevention.* New York: Plenum, 1990.

EMIL J. POSAVAC is professor of psychology at Loyola University of Chicago.

A decision maker who uses program evaluations in an educational setting identifies four types of evaluation misuse and provides two case studies in which evaluators misused their positions and the evaluations by not modifying research questions that were determined to be inappropriate.

Evaluation Misuse from a User's Perspective

Carla J. Stevens

Discussions regarding the issue of evaluation misuse often focus on misuse by the user as the recipient of the evaluation results. Misuse can also occur on the part of the evaluator and the role he or she plays in the evaluation process. The evaluator must take an active role throughout the evaluation in order to accurately assess both the formal and informal objectives of a program.

This chapter addresses the issue of evaluation misuse from the perspective of the user. It is the result of an interview with an assistant superintendent of a large urban school district regarding experiences she has had with evaluations. She has been involved in the development and management of a number of programs for at-risk children and families. This chapter represents her opinions and experiences as a user in the evaluation process.

Misuse from a User's Perspective

The first misuse of evaluation is not misuse of data but the nonuse of evaluators at the beginning to help formulate questions that can actually be evaluated or measured. That is the greatest misuse by program personnel at the start. Too many people rely on what they think are standard measures for judging whether something is successful and they do not look at the fact that those measures are not directly affected by the impact of the program. These standard measures are grandiose items such as academic achievement and self-esteem.

Another misuse is that the evaluator does not speak up strongly and clearly in the planning phase of the program and during evaluation design. Although they are involved with the program people in the planning phase, evaluators see themselves as separate and do not steer the program people in the right direction. Program people tend to jump on certain bandwagons. It is typical to pick items such as academic achievement and self-esteem to be improved, no matter what the direct impact of the program may be. Very often, evaluators do not help people structure the evaluation questions clearly enough with a dose of reality, making sure that what they say they will measure is actually measurable and is a direct outcome of the program.

A third misuse that occurs is that the original research questions are not the right ones, and once this fact is discovered, they are not exchanged for more appropriate ones. They seem like the right ones in the planning phase because they are fairly traditional. Often, however, both the people planning programs and the evaluators do not have a lot of experience. They plan the program as they wish it would be, but they do not have the experience of going through a long-term project with multiple intervention strategies that are trying to effect some sort of systemic change. This is partly because people seldom have opportunities to become involved in large, long-term projects. However, in recent years, funders have pushed for more programs based on multifaceted, collaborative models with involvement from various populations in an attempt to effect systemic change.

Often, the evaluators on the front lines are fairly new and naïve. When program evaluators get more experience and become good at what they do, they move up to administrative roles. The experienced evaluators are most often not those working in the trenches with the program personnel. Furthermore, very few evaluators are trained regarding the evaluation of complex programs using multiple intervention strategies in naturalistic settings.

A fourth misuse on the part of evaluators may occur when cultural differences are not seriously taken into account in designing the program evaluation. For example, if one of the program goals was to improve parent involvement, the evaluator would have to look at different measures for a school in a predominantly African-American community than for a school in a largely Hispanic community. For one school, you might want to measure how many more times a parent comes to school and is *not* verbally demanding, but at another school, you would measure how many times they come to school and *are* demanding. With one group, if they come to school and make a demand, that would be an improvement. With another group, if they come to school and do not make a demand, that would be an improvement. In addition to cultural biases, there are also neighborhood biases. You can have one school with a 95 percent African-American student population and have very different kinds of parents than in another school with a 95 percent African-American population. Thus, in designing research questions and developing measures to collect data, evaluators must remember to be sensitive to not only the needs of the program staff but also to the characteristics of the target population.

The following case studies address the third type of evaluation misuse: not modifying the original research question to adequately reflect what is actually happening in the program.

Program Example One: Federally Funded Dropout Prevention Demonstration Project

The first case study involves a federally funded dropout prevention demonstration project. It was based on a program originally implemented in San Antonio, Texas. The program had a component where at-risk junior and senior high school students were trained to be tutors of at-risk middle school students. The original program talked about the changes in the tutors as well as the tutees. In designing the district's demonstration project, the program personnel read all that, knew all that, and yet had not written research questions to capture changes in the tutors. Measures were still not applied to the tutor changes although dramatic changes were being observed with the tutors and virtually nothing was happening with the tutees. Because the tutors were not the target population, any effect on them was considered merely a side effect and not a program outcome. In reality, change in the tutors is exactly what was found in the original program as well.

The initial question was quite convoluted and had nothing to do with what the demonstration project actually did. Furthermore, it did not address program effects on the junior and senior high school tutors. However, the question remained in writing, and when the evaluators conducted the evaluation, they went on doggedly answering this question, which made absolutely no sense in light of the program. Consequently, the results of the evaluation were useless.

From a user's perspective, the purpose of program evaluation is to tell program staff how to do things better. It is to inform decision makers of improvements needed in the decision-making and planning process, far more than it is to measure academic success or improvements in attendance. Thus, one of the biggest failings of evaluators is to hang on to an evaluation plan as if they were doing some scientific experiment. Program evaluation people tend to come out of a strong empirical mode where they doggedly must follow the path they have chosen to the end. This was true in this case. Although it was apparent that the research question was not the right question, the evaluators continued to answer it instead of writing a paragraph saying, "We asked the wrong question," and then discussing actual program outcomes they observed.

This same type of evaluation misuse occurred at the national level with this project. The national grant was initially funded for a three-year period. Large demonstration grants were awarded all over the United States with a significant amount of money committed to the national evaluation. The Department of Education hired a research group from California to design the evaluation. They designed an evaluation that did not fit most of the programs, especially the one implemented in the district. They had little or no direct contact with the actual program sites during the design and data collection phases. The kind of data you get when you ask people to fill out forms is useless because of too many misunderstandings and questions about the forms. This is where program people begin to question the results. "The evaluators never came, they did not talk to us, they just sent us this form to fill out, and the form did not fit the program activities. How can they tell us our program is not working, when we see results on a daily basis?" That is what happened with the national evaluation for this program, as it has with other nationally evaluated programs.

Furthermore, the program came up for review and was funded for another four years by the federal government, before the national evaluators presented any data or evaluation report. When the new request for proposals was sent out for the additional four years of funding, it was identical to the first one. It was as if nothing had been learned in three years of program operation, and, at that point, this was true because the evaluation report was not completed.

A similar situation occurred locally. When it was time to write the proposal for the additional four years' funding, the local evaluation report was not finished due to the three-month lag time in dropout data. The program people wrote what they thought was effective in the program, and based resources and commitment to personnel on that. A summer program component was left out that had taken a lot of work to implement. However, once the evaluation was received, it showed that the component that made the most difference on dropout rates was the one left out of the funding proposal. The other components, such as the interventions of social workers and diagnosticians, had not made any directly discernible differences in these at-risk students' academic achievement or dropout rates. Yet, the summer program that oriented the middle school students to high school showed far greater retention rates for these students during high school than for similar students who did not participate in the summer orientation component. If the evaluators who had been with the program since its inception were getting a sense of which components were working and which were not, they should have let the program personnel know earlier.

Program Example Two: University-Based Multicommunity Initiative

A second example of misuse by asking the wrong research question revolves around a university-based multicommunity initiative to improve school–community relations. The project evaluation plan was designed by a very large group of individuals. In fact, it involved more evaluators than program people because it was based at a university. With both this and the previously described program, the evaluators were with the program people all along; they came to the meetings, they were at the schools doing direct data collection, they were working with the service providers, and they designed the forms jointly. It was the ideal collaboration between program people and evaluators. All along, they listened as people talked about and described what they were seeing, and yet they never helped or changed the initial research questions or program objectives to capture what was really happening with the program and the participants.

The thrust of the program was to increase parents' involvement in their children's education by making the school the locus of many different kinds of support services for families. It was funded by a foundation for mental health, so most of the areas targeted were mental health issues.

In reality, what parents wanted were not mental health services. What started happening was that parents became involved in the school, which had been a spoken goal of the program since its inception, but was never articulated as a research goal such that anybody was collecting any data. Whenever the program people, including the evaluation team, met, they talked about the tremendous changes in parents. These changes were things that could be measured, such as attendance at school functions, frequency of interaction with other parents, frequency of accepting roles in the school, and involvement in school activities such as the carnival. The observable outcome of the program was that parents were becoming more comfortable and had more ownership in the school. This was something that the program people felt was very important, yet it was not captured in the evaluation because they did not ask those questions up front or talk about them beforehand. The evaluators went on with the original questions even though they knew increased parental involvement was a major goal of the program.

The main problem in these two examples is that although the evaluators were with the program the entire time and knew what was going on with the program participants, the evaluation did not reflect the actual program outcomes. Sometimes the intent of the program is not articulated well enough at first, possibly because it is difficult to anticipate what you are going to see. Once certain outcomes are observed, and you know that they meet the intent of the program, the evaluation team should be flexible enough to modify the evaluation plan and design measures that capture those changes. Otherwise, the information provided is useless, and the evaluators have misused their position on the team, the resources distributed to the evaluation, and the time of the program personnel and participants.

Advice from a User

At the very onset of a program, the evaluators must not only be involved, but take an active role in the design of the program goals, research questions, and evaluation plan. They must give a dose of reality about what change program people can honestly expect. The evaluator has to speak up.

The second piece of advice to evaluators is to write evaluation questions that are of value to the program people. Help program people see that this long-term question, academic achievement, is not what will help them make decisions about the program. Even the federal government and other funders do not seem to be asking for totally rigid outcome-based evaluations any more. They seem to be quite comfortable with process reports. Evaluations should be more process-oriented to give valuable design and decision-making information to people who are doing the program. Furthermore, the evaluation must reflect the actual activities of the program, not just the originally stated goals of the program designers.

There may be many ways to misuse an evaluation. Not asking the right questions, and then when you realize that you are not, being unwilling to change is a serious misuse from a program person's perspective. This inability to move with the program and to ask the questions that are really emerging rather than staying with the original questions is a major failing of evaluation.

CARLA J. STEVENS is president of Evaluation & Data Analysis Services, Inc., Houston, Texas.

INDEX

85

Program sponsors, 8, 9, 17. *See also* Stakeholders
Program staff, 9, 12, 41, 76; fear of evaluation, 70; self-interests of, 10, 63; *See also* Stakeholders
Project NITCUN, case study of, 50–59
Propriety standards. *See* Standards

Raizen, S. A., 67
Rein, M., 49, 55
Research questions, 80, 81, 82, 83
Resource deficiencies, 34, 35, 43
Richardson, E. L., 33
Roessner, J., 77
Rossi, P. H., 3, 8, 10, 15, 16, 20, 67, 73
Rossi's Iron Law of Evaluation, 15–16
Rothman, R., 66
Rutman, L., 49, 57

Scriven, M., 70
Senge, P. M., 44, 45
Sessions, W. S., 29
Shadish, W. R., Jr., 3, 4, 10, 11,16, 19, 20.
Simmons, B. P., 71
Smukler, M., 34, 45
Sonnichsen, R. C., 25, 28, 34, 45
Special interest groups, 37–39

Special population committees, 39
Spector, M., 20
Spergel, I., 17
Stakeholders: assumptions of, about evaluations, 69, 77; definition of, 8; and evaluation results, 7; power of, over evaluator, 6; program-level, 69, 70, 71, 76; self-interests of, 66; and standards, 5.
Standards, 5, 6, 8, 12
Stevens, C. J., 9, 11
Summative evaluation, 7, 9, 71–72, 76, 77; limitations of, 74; misunderstanding of, 73, 75; need for, 72

Target participants, 9, 11. *See also* Stakeholders
Taylor, S. E., 70

Utility standards. *See* Standards

Vroom, P. I., 7, 9, 10, 12

Webster, W. H., 29
Weiss, C. H., 8, 19, 49, 59
Weiss, R., 49, 55
Weisse, C. S. ,75
Wildavsky, A., 21
Wye, C., 34, 45

NEW DIRECTIONS FOR PROGRAM EVALUATION, no. 63, Fall 1994   © Jossey-Bass Publishers

ERRATUM

A corrected version of Figure 1.1 (page 15) appears below. In the published version, the numbers 11, 13, 15, 17, and 19 had been left out of the "low-intensity control" random assignment scenario. These numbers are included below in boldface.

Figure 1.1. Perception of Random Misassignment

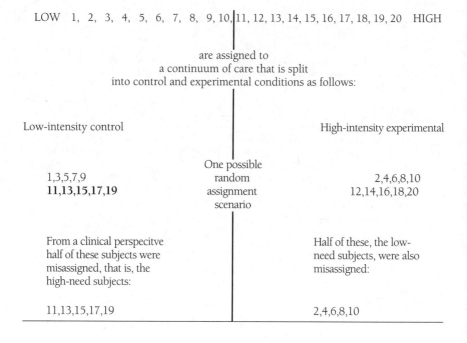

Twenty eligible subjects arranged on a
continuum of need

LOW   1,   2,   3,   4,   5,   6,   7,   8,   9, 10, 11, 12, 13, 14, 15, 16, 17, 18, 19, 20   HIGH

are assigned to
a continuum of care that is split
into control and experimental conditions as follows:

Low-intensity control   High-intensity experimental

	One possible	
1,3,5,7,9	random	2,4,6,8,10
11,13,15,17,19	assignment	12,14,16,18,20
	scenario	

From a clinical perspecitve   Half of these, the low-
half of these subjects were   need subjects, were also
misassigned, that is, the   misassigned:
high-need subjects:

11,13,15,17,19   2,4,6,8,10

ORDERING INFORMATION

NEW DIRECTIONS FOR PROGRAM EVALUATION is a series of paperback books that presents the latest techniques and procedures for conducting useful evaluation studies of all types of programs. Books in the series are published quarterly in Spring, Summer, Fall, and Winter and are available for purchase by subscription as well as by single copy.

SUBSCRIPTIONS for 1994 cost $54.00 for individuals (a savings of 34 percent over single-copy prices) and $75.00 for institutions, agencies, and libraries. Please do not send institutional checks for personal subscriptions. Standing orders are accepted.

SINGLE COPIES cost $17.95 when payment accompanies order. (California, New Jersey, New York, and Washington, D.C., residents please include appropriate sales tax.) Billed orders will be charged postage and handling.

DISCOUNTS FOR QUANTITY ORDERS are available. Please write to the address below for information.

ALL ORDERS must include either the name of an individual or an official purchase order number. Please submit your order as follows:
Subscriptions: specify series and year subscription is to begin
Single copies: include individual title code (such as PE59)

MAIL ALL ORDERS TO:
Jossey-Bass Publishers
350 Sansome Street
San Francisco, California 94104-1342

FOR SUBSCRIPTION SALES OUTSIDE OF THE UNITED STATES, CONTACT:
any international subscription agency or Jossey-Bass directly.

OTHER TITLES AVAILABLE IN THE
NEW DIRECTIONS FOR PROGRAM EVALUATION SERIES
William R. Shadish, Editor-in-Chief